Studying the Novel

An Introduction

JEREMY HAWTHORN
Professor of Modern British Literature
University of Trondheim, Norway

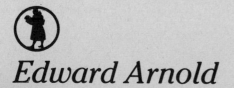

Edward Arnold

First published in Great Britain 1985 by
Edward Arnold (Publishers) Ltd, 41 Bedford Square,
London WC1B 3DQ

Edward Arnold (Australia) Pty Ltd, 80 Waverley Road,
Caulfield East, Victoria 3145, Australia

British Library Cataloguing in Publication Data

Hawthorn, Jeremy
  Studying the novel: an introduction.
  1. Fiction   2. Criticism
  I. Title
  801′.953   PN3335

  ISBN 0–7131–6449–2

Text set in 10/11pt Cheltenham Book Compugraphic
by Colset Private Ltd, Singapore
Printed and bound in Great Britain by
Richard Clay (The Chaucer Press) Ltd, Bungay, Suffolk

Contents

1 Introductory Definitions

According to the Oxford English dictionary a novel is 'a fictitious prose narrative or tale of considerable length (now usually one long enough to fill one or more volumes) in which characters and actions representative of the real life of past or present times are portrayed in a plot of more or less complexity.'

This may sound a bit like stating the obvious, but there are some important points contained in this very concise definition.

The novel is fictitious – *fiction*, as we often refer to it. It depicts imaginary characters and situations. A novel may include reference to real places, people and events, but it cannot contain only such references and remain a novel. However, even though its characters and actions are imaginary they are in some sense 'representative of real life' as the dictionary definition has it; although fictional they bear an important resemblance to the real. What exactly this resemblance is has been a matter of much discussion and dispute amongst literary critics, and it is arguable that it varies in kind from novel to novel. But this resemblance to *real* life is one of the features that distinguishes the novel from other forms such as the epic and the romance, however much we recognize that the term 'real life' is a problematic concept that requires careful definition and use.

The novel is in *prose* rather than verse, although novels can well include very 'poetic' elements so far as their language is concerned. And although it would be a serious mistake to assume that the language of a novel was identical to ordinary speech or most non-literary writing, nevertheless the fact that the novel is in prose helps to establish that sense of 'real

life' – of recognizable everyday existence – that is the preserve of the genre.

The novel is a *narrative*: in other words it is in some sense a
'telling' rather than an 'enacting', and this distinguishes it in an
important sense from the drama. Of course novels can contain
very dramatic scenes, and often the reader may forget that
what we learn of character and event is not direct (as in the
theatre or the cinema) but mediated through a particular
telling, a narrative source. Take the opening of Henry James's
short story 'The Lesson of the Master' (1888):

He had been told the ladies were at church, but this was corrected by
what he saw from the top of the steps – they descended from a great
height in two arms, with a circular sweep of the most charming
effect – at the threshold of the door which, from the long bright
gallery, overlooked the immense lawn.

If our first impression is that we are witnessing a scene directly,
a second glance will confirm that we are actually being *told*
about the scene. The telling is such that we can visualize what
is described – that is often the mark of an accomplished narrative – but we see what is pointed out to us by a narrator or a
narrative voice or source. In a filmed version of this scene the
different members of the cinema audience could choose to
concentrate upon different aspects of what unfolded before
them; the reader of James's short story, in contrast, 'sees' what
James's narrator chooses that he or she shall see. And how
would a film director convey that 'he' had been told something
earlier, while leaving us absolutely in the dark at this point with
regard to who 'he' is, what he looks like, and who told him
about the ladies being at church?

Moreover, the novel has *characters, actions(s)*, and a *plot*: it
involves people who do things in a total context ruled over by
some sort of connective logic: chronology, cause-and-effect, or
whatever. There is, moreover, in most novels a connection
between these three elements such that they form some sort of
unity. A poem does not have to contain characters or a plot or
indeed action, but it is only very rare novels which dispense
with one of these elements, and in such unusual cases it is often
a matter of dispute as to whether the net result is recognizable
as a novel. As Ian Watt has pointed out, too, the novel is
distinguished by the fact that unlike the works of the great

English and Classical poets and dramatists its plots are generally not taken from traditional sources.[1]

And finally, the novel is of a certain length. A poem can be
anything from a couplet to a thousand pages or more, but we
feel unhappy about granting the term 'novel' to a tale of some
forty or fifty pages. Of course it is not just a question of length:
we feel that a novel should involve a investigation of an issue of
human significance in such a manner as allows for complexity
of treatment, and by common consent a certain length is necessary to allow for such complexity. In practice, therefore, we
usually refer to a prose narrative of some twenty or thirty
pages or less as a short story, while works that seem to hover
on the awkward boundary between 'short story' and 'novel',
having a length of between forty or fifty and a hundred pages,
we describe as novellas.

2   The History of the Novel

Studying the emergence of the novel is a little like reading one of those historical accounts of the emergence of the human species; all sorts of near-misses occur, dead-ends of development peter out, and then – miraculously – all the required ingredients come together and human beings come into being. And just as researchers are still arguing about 'disputed ancestors' of the human species (are we or are we not descended from this particular ape-like creature?), so too literary critics and historians are by no means in total agreement about the ancestors of the novel. We do, however, know rather more about the birth of the novel than we know or are likely ever to know about the emergence of the human species.

Fictional narratives can be found almost as far back as we have written records, but these lack many of the characteristics that today we associate with the novel. Firstly, they are normally in verse rather than prose. Secondly, they do not concern themselves with 'the real life of past or present times' but portray the life of gods or mythical heroes whose lives can hardly be said to resemble 'real life' (however it is defined) except in extremely indirect ways.

We have to be careful here, however, because one of the important traditions which contributes to the emergence of the novel is that of the *romance* – as the term 'roman', which is the equivalent of 'novel' in many modern European languages, reveals. (The word 'novel' comes, confusingly, from the Italian 'novella' – 'small new thing'.) The chivalric romance developed in twelfth-century France and depicted not epic heroes but a highly stylized and idealized courtly life founded upon rigid but sophisticated conventions of behaviour. Like the epic (which it displaced) it often involved supernatural elements –

another factor which in general terms distinguishes it from the modern novel. The eighteenth-century man of politics Lord Chesterfield, writing to his son about the novel, describes it in terms that make its relation to the romance clear.

I am in doubt whether you know what a Novel is: it is a little gallant history, which must contain a great deal of love, and not exceed one or two small volumes. The subject must be a love affair; the lovers are to meet with many difficulties and obstacles, to oppose the accomplishment of their wishes, but at last overcome them all; and the conclusion or catastrophe must leave them happy. A Novel is a kind of abbreviation of a Romance; for a Romance generally consists of twelve volumes, all filled with insipid love nonsense, and most incredible adventures.

. . .

In short, the reading of Romances is a most frivolous occupation, and time merely thrown away. The old Romances, written two or three hundred years ago, such as Amadis of Gaul, Orlando the Furious, and others, were stuffed with enchantments, magicians, giants, and such sort of impossibilities, whereas the more modern Romances keep within the bounds of possibility, but not of probability.[2]

Chesterfields's comments are interesting not just from the connection he claims between the romance and the novel, but also from the light that they throw upon the relatively low status that the novel enjoyed in its early years. We should remember that even when the study of English literature was introduced into British universities in the early part of the twentieth century it was expected that this would in the main be limited to the drama and to poetry. Chesterfield was of course an aristocrat, with an education that had steeped him in classical learning. As I will be pointing out below the novel was associated not with the aristocracy but with the rising middle class in the century of its birth, and often with people lacking the classical learning of Chesterfield.

Although for our immediate purposes it is important to distinguish the novel from the romance, it has to be remembered that the novel superseded the romance by, to a certain extent, incorporating some important elements of the romance in itself. Thus there is a recognizable line of development in the novel which often reminds us of aspects of the romance, from the gothic novel through science fiction to fantasy works such as *The Lord of the Rings* (1954). (See Chapter 3 following.)

The English critic Arnold Kettle in his excellent introductory book on the novel suggests that most novelists in their approach to writing show a bias towards either 'life' or 'pattern': towards, in other words, either the aim to convey the vividness and feel of living, or that of conveying some interpretation of the significance of life. According to Kettle the novelist who starts with pattern often tries to 'inject' life into it, while the novelist who starts with life tries to make a pattern emerge out of it. He relates these two very general tendencies to, on the one hand, such sources and influences as the parables of the Bible, the Morality plays of the Middle Ages, and the sermons which common people listened to every Sunday ('pattern'), and on the other hand to the seventeenth and early eighteenth century prose journalism and pamphleteering of such as Thomas Nashe and Daniel Defoe (who, we should remember, was a political journalist before he was a novelist). As Kettle says of such writers, the germ of their books is never an idea, never an abstract concept; they are 'less consciously concerned with the moral significance of life than with its surface texture'.[3]

If we remember that the novel is essentially a telling – a narrative – we can perhaps see why there are these lines of development in the novel, not crudely or obviously present of course, but recognizable still today in the difference between a novel like Kingsley Amis's *Lucky Jim* (1954) and William Golding's *Lord of the Flies* (1954). When we tell someone a story, whether it's about a traffic accident in which we were involved or the history of the boy scout movement, we normally have to make a decision about whether we will concentrate upon conveying what it felt like to be lying in the road with a broken leg, or to be a boy scout in 1923; or whether we will concentrate on making a *point* – about the driver's carelessness, or the health-giving effect of listening to songs round the camp-fire from a water-logged tent, or whatever. It is perhaps the mark of the greatest novels that with them it is most difficult to say whether or not the novelist has tried more to convey 'life' or 'pattern', for both seem so consumately present.

The emergence of the novel

The novel is a young genre, a tiny infant indeed in comparison to poetry and drama, both of which seem to be about as old as humanity. The novel emerges in its recognizably modern form in the Europe of the eighteenth century. Crucial to its development are a number of rather different factors, of which it is worth stressing four in particular.

(i) The rise of *literacy*. The novel is essentially a written form, unlike poetry which exists for centuries prior to the development of writing, and still flourishes in oral cultures today. There have been cases of illiterate people gathering to hear novels read – part of Dickens's audience was of this sort – and during the Victorian period the habit of reading aloud within the family was much more widespread than it is today. But the novel is typically *written* by one individual in private and read silently by another.

(ii) *Printing*: the modern novel is the child of the printing press, which alone can produce the vast numbers of copies needed to satisfy a literate public at a price that they can afford. This factor means also that the relationship between the novelist and his or her readers is a relatively anonymous one; the novelist does not know his or her readers personally, nor has direct contact with them. Typically the novel is read *in private* by an individual. Experiencing a novel is thus a much less collective and public matter than experiencing a performed play can be, where we are very conscious of how the rest of the audience is reacting.

(iii) A *market economy*. The 'sociology of the novel' is based very much upon a market relationship between author and reader mediated through publishers. In contrast to earlier methods of financing publication or supporting authors such as patronage (a rich patron would support a writer while he was writing) or subscription (rich potential readers would subscribe money to support a writer in order that he might write a particular work), a market economy increases the relative freedom and isolation of the writer and decreases his immediate dependence upon particular individuals, groups, or interests. The growth of a market economy is of course an aspect of the rise of capitalism – the system which had displaced feudalism in Britain by the eighteenth century. In his book *The Rise of the Novel* (1957) Ian Watt has argued for a close relationship between the rise of the novel and the rise of the middle class, and in different ways literacy, printing and a market economy can all be related to the establishment of capitalism in the period during which the novel emerges. But probably the most crucial development (for the creation of the novel) brought about by capitalism is my fourth point.

(iv) The rise of *individualism*. Ian Watt sees as typical of the novel that it includes 'individualization of ... characters and ... the detailed presentation of their environment'. Unlike many of the narratives that precede it the novel does not just present us with 'type' characters; we are interested in Tom Jones, David Copperfield, Maggie Tulliver and Paul Morel as distinct individuals with personal qualities and idiosyncrasies. As Ralph Fox puts it, somewhat tendentiously,

The novel deals with the individual, it is the epic of the struggle of the individual against society, against nature, and it could only develop in a society where the balance between man and society was lost, where man was at war with his fellows or with nature. Such a society is capitalist society.[4]

Fox exemplifies his argument by contrasting the *Odyssey* with *Robinson Crusoe* (1719), pointing out that whereas Odysseus lives in a society without history and knows that his fate is in the hands of the gods, Robinson Crusoe is prepared to make his own history. Moreover, whereas Odysseus's efforts are directed towards returning *home*, for Crusoe it is the outward and not the homeward trip that is important, he is 'the man who challenges nature and wins'. Crusoe is thus, for Fox, representative of that spirit of expansionism, self-reliance and experimentation that characterizes early capitalist man.

It certainly seems to be the case that the new spirit that accompanies the early development of capitalism infuses the emerging novel. Along with a stress on individualism goes, too, a growing concern with the inner self, the private life, subjective experience. As the individual *feels* him or herself an individual, rather than a member of a static feudal community with duties and characteristics which are endowed at birth, then he or she starts more to think in terms of having certain purely personal rather than merely communal interests. And this gives the individual something to *hide*. Without wishing to oversimplify an extremely complex and far from uniform historical development we can say that in a certain sense the private life as we know it today is born with capitalist society, and that the novel both responds and contributes to this development. Of all literary genres the novel most consummately unites an exploration of the subjective and the social, of the private and the collective. The lyric poem has offered us highly personal statements of individual feeling and cerebration, but without the ability to contextualize these in the manner of the novel's detailed depiction of the complex relationships between subjective feeling and history and society. Drama has provided us with human beings interacting within the pressures of a given society at a particular time, but its most sophisticated verbal portrayals of subjective experience – Hamlet's soliloquys, for instance – are technically crude in comparison to what the novel can achieve in this direction. Even the simplicity of that opening sentence from James's 'The Lesson of the Master' gives us something that is beyond the scope of the lyric poem and the drama (or film). It is this combination of the broadest social and historical sweep with the most acute and penetrating visions of the hidden, private life, *and their interconnections*, that is characteristic of the novel and at the heart of its power and continuing life.

Moreover, although the novel is both written and read in private, it relies upon a highly organized society and industry to produce and circulate it. Even in its sociology it combines the personal and the social, that combination that is at the heart of its aesthetic.

It is possible that the early association of the novel with town rather than country life may well have something to do with this unique combination. There are novels set in the country of course, but from its earliest days the novel appears to have had a special relationship with town life. If we look at what has a fair claim to be one of the first modern novels – Daniel Defoe's *Moll Flanders* (1722) we can see that the town and the novel form have much in common. Both involve large numbers of people leading interdependent lives, influencing and relying upon one another, but each possessing, nevertheless, a core of private thoughts and personal goals.

It is interesting, however, to note that from its earliest days the novel seems to split not just between novels where the author starts with 'life' and those in which the author starts with 'pattern', but between novels in which the author is more interested in the public world and novels in which the author is more interested in private life. Again, it is only the very greatest novels that seem to combine the two such that we feel no sense of subordination of either. Henry Fielding's *Tom Jones* (1749) and Samuel Richardson's *Clarissa* (1747–8) can be taken as representative here, with the former's greater interest in a masculine, public life of movement, action and life in the larger social world in sharp contrast to the latter's concentration upon a feminine, more inward life of feeling, personal relationships, and personal moral decision. This is not to deny that Fielding's novel includes a concern with feeling and moral duty and Richardson's with the larger social context of the inner world. But nonetheless there is a significant difference between the two writers' foci of interest, a difference which is perceptively brought out in a conversation reported by James Boswell in his *The Life of Samuel Johnson*, which was first published in 1791. Talking to Johnson and Thomas Erskine, Boswell expressed surprise at Johnson's calling Fielding a 'blockhead' and 'a barren rascal'.

BOSWELL. 'Will you not allow, Sir, that he draws very natural pictures of human life?' JOHNSON. 'Why, Sir, it is of very low life. Richardson used to say, that had he not known who Fielding was, he should have believed he was an ostler. Sir, there is more knowledge of the heart in one letter of Richardson's, than in all *Tom Jones*. . . . ERSKINE. 'Surely, Sir, Richardson is very tedious.' JOHNSON. 'Why, Sir, if you were to read Richardson for the story, your impatience would be so much fretted that you would hang yourself. But you must read him for the sentiment, and consider the story as only giving occasion to the sentiment.' [Anecdote from year 1772]

We do not need to accept Johnson's value judgements to feel the force of the distinction made here, between a primary interest in drawing very natural pictures of life – albeit low life – and that of revealing knowledge of the human heart.

I talked earlier about Fielding's interest in the masculine and Richardson's in the feminine sphere, and I should make it clear that this is a historical rather than a universal judgement; 'masculine' and 'feminine' as they were defined by eighteenth-century English society, in which men were able to live a public as well as a domestic life, a public life of travel, work, exploration and adventure. The relationship of women to the novel is a very important one, however, which ought to be touched upon at this stage. This importance is both as writers and as readers. Although the early novelists in England and elsewhere are predominantly men up until the late eighteenth century, women soon formed a substantial and, on occasions, a dominant section of the reading public. This, of course, because of the market economy on which novel production depended, had an appreciable effect upon the sort of novels that were written, and it is impossible to imagine Richardson's novels having been written as they were without a substantial female reading public.

But by the nineteenth century women are a dominant element not just as readers but as writers of the novel. What male novelist is there then to compare with Jane Austen, Emily Brontë and George Eliot in England, apart from Charles Dickens? It is arguable that the novel's success in exploring the private world, the subjective self, could never have been accomplished without the contribution to the genre of that introspective self-knowledge and sensitive perception of inter-personal relations that women's domestic imprisonment had trained them to be so expert in. No man could have written Jane Austen's novels.

Perhaps we can add another point to our list of the novel's achievements: no other literary genre has enriched itself so fully and so impartially from the culture and experience of both sexes. (Which is not, of course, to say that the novel is innocent of the blinkered vision and perceptual shortcomings of women or, especially, of men.)

3 Types of Novel

Categorizing novels may seem rather a tedious and mechanical procedure, but it is alas a fact that we can badly misread (and thus fail to extract the value and pleasure from our reading that we could have enjoyed) if we mistake the type of novel that we are reading. As my previously quoted comment from Johnson on Richardson suggests, one can approach a novel in such an inappropriate way as a result of misperceiving the sort of novel that it is, that one may end up 'so much fretted' that one feels suicidal! Interestingly, Johnson is commenting upon a near-contemporary of his in Richardson: the fact that we are reading a novel written in our own lifetime is no guarantee that we will understand the sort of novel that it is. But the danger of such a mistaken approach certainly increases when we read novels from an earlier time, novels written for readers with assumptions and expectations which we may not share.

Novels can be categorized both historically and technically, and in practice these two elements tend to overlap as particular types of novel often flourish within defined historical boundaries. What follows is a list of some of the most commonly used categories, with some explanation and discussion of the terms used to denote these categories.

These categorizations should be used as a guide rather than a strait-jacket: no novel is *just* a picaresque novel or a bildungsroman. Every novel has something creative and unique in itself, every novel (and some much more than others) challenges the expectations and assumptions of readers to a certain extent.

The picaresque novel

A 'picaro' in Spanish is a rogue, and the picaresque novel is built on the tradition of the sixteenth-century Spanish picaresque narrative, which typically portrayed a sharp-witted rogue living off his wits while travelling through a variety of usually low-life settings. Recent commentators have suggested that the key aspect of the picaro is that he is a minor delinquent who offends against moral and civil laws and whose behaviour is anti-social without being utterly vicious. The picaro typically lives by begging or by minor theft, he is cynical in his attitude to the softer emotions, especially love, and by witty and satirical comments questions most established beliefs and customs. Critics frequently relate the emergence of the picaro to the break-up of the feudal world, and his open-minded, self-interested, geographical and intellectual wandering and questing are seen by many to merge into the spirit of possessive individualism that is ushered in with the growth of capitalist social relations.

The picaresque novel is typically *episodic*, and it normally lacks a sophisticated plot or psychologically complex or developing characters.

Daniel Defoe's novel *Moll Flanders* is by no means a pure picaresque novel; quite apart from anything else the fact that its main character is a woman represents a significant divergence from previous picaresque novels. But it is possessed of many typical characteristics of the picaresque novel. It is constructed around a sequence of short 'episodes' none of which is longer than two or three pages, and it has little real development of character (Moll repents when she is facing execution, but this seems based on no fundamental *change* in her character or values.)

There is debate concerning the term 'picaresque novel' (as with many other such terms) as to whether the term should be defined narrowly or in a more catholic manner. Thus in a certain sense one can say that only a small number of sixteenth-century Spanish works are truly picaresque; in a much wider sense one can say that there are picaresque elements in a recent novel like Kingsley Amis's *Lucky Jim*.

Whatever one's decision regarding usage here, it remains the case that the picaresque tradition makes a very important contribution to the development of the novel, providing a model for ways to introduce variety and suspense in to the genre, and indicating that there are no social experiences that are out of bounds to the novel.

The epistolary novel

An epistolary novel is told through letters ('epistles') exchanged between different characters. It flourished in particular in the eighteenth century, and Samuel Richardson's *Pamela* (1740) and *Clarissa*; Tobias Smollett's *Humphry Clinker* (1771); and Fanny Burney's *Evelina* (1778) are classic epistolary novels.

Given how important letters were in English society in the eighteenth century, when literacy was high amongst educated people but transport facilities were very primitive by modern standards, it is not surprising that the novel should be heavily influenced by this form of communication in its early development. In his novel *Clarissa* Samuel Richardson gives a comment to his character Mr Belfield, writing to Lovelace about Clarissa, which helps to explain the attraction to the author of the epistolary technique:

Such a sweetness of temper, so much patience and resignation, as she seems to be mistress of; yet writing of and in the midst of *present* distresses! How *much more* lively and affecting, for that reason, must her style be, her mind tortured by the pangs of uncertainty (the events then hidden in the womb of fate), *than* the dry narrative, unanimated style of a person relating difficulties and dangers surmounted; the relater perfectly at ease; and if himself unmoved by his own story, not likely greatly to affect the reader.[5]

Clearly the personal insight, self-display, and dramatic effectiveness of the epistolary technique are what appeal to Richardson. But a novel told exclusively through letters (Richardson allows himself the occasional authorial footnote and square-bracketed interpolation!) can be unwieldy and inflexible. The characters have to be kept apart (otherwise they have no reason to write to one another), and sometimes this involves artificiality: Richardson's heroines are banished to locked rooms with disturbing regularity. And when they actually meet their loved ones Richardson has somehow to arrange for someone else to write a letter about the encounter.

Moreover, whatever else the characters do they must always have access to pen and paper; just as the subjects of Browning's dramatic monologues cannot be allowed to lose their voices, so too Richardson's heroines must keep writing. As Clarissa on one occasion writes to Miss Howe: 'And indeed, my dear, I know not how to *forbear* writing. I have now no other employment or diversion. And I must write on, although I were not to send it to anybody.' It was this element in Richardson's *Pamela* that was so cruelly but effectively satirized by Henry Fielding in his parody *Shamela*,* in which the heroine continues to write a letter while the man who is assaulting her virtue climbs into bed with her.

If the 'pure' epistolary novel is rare after the eighteenth century (although there are, every now and then, such novels still being written), the form taught novelists how very useful letters could be as an element within the narrative variety of a novel. Think how useful it is to Emily Brontë to be able to include Isabella's long letter about her marriage to Heathcliff in *Wuthering Heights* (1847), and how perfectly Helen's letters to her sister contribute to E.M. Forster's *Howards End* (1910). But perhaps the most important thing that later novelists were able to learn from the epistolary novel was that it is unwise to strait-jacket a novelist by the choice of too restrictive or inflexible a narrative technique, and as we shall see later on, the post-eighteenth-century novel generally displays a far greater flexibility of narrative technique than is to be found in the classic epistolary novel.

The historical novel

As its name suggests the historical novel sets its events and characters in a well-defined historical context, and it may include both fictional and real characters. It is often distinguished (in its more respectable forms) by convincing detailed description of the manners, building, institutions and scenery of its chosen setting, and generally attempts to convey a sense of historical verisimilitude. Its most respected practitioner in Britain has been Sir Walter Scott.

In its more recent popular, 'pulp' form it tends to abandon verisimilitude for fantasy, and in some ways can be seen as the

---

* The full title is: *An Apology for the Life of Mrs Shamela Andrews* (1741).

present-day version of the romance, encouraging more an escape from reality than a critical and imaginative scrutiny of it.

The regional novel

The regional novel involves an especial focus of attention on to the life of a particular, well-defined geographical region. Traditionally the region in question will be rural rather than urban (thus it would be distinctly odd to refer to Charles Dickens as a regional novelist, in spite of the fact that so many of his novels explore London life in such intimate detail). Very often a 'regional novelist' will write a number of books all involving the same territory or place – as with Thomas Hardy's 'Wessex' and William Faulkner's 'Yoknapatawpha County'. Both of these 'regions' are closely modelled on particular areas of England and the United States, in spite of their fictitious names (and, ironically, the popularity of Hardy's novels has led to the term 'Wessex' being used to denote that part of England upon which it is based).

Whether we feel happy about calling a novelist a regional novelist may well depend upon our view of his or her stature: to many the term has a rather limiting ring, and this leads them to reserve use of it for indisputably minor novelists.

The satirical novel

Satire does not have to be either in prose or to be fictional, although there is a sense in which the exaggeration upon which it typically depends necessarily involves a certain amount of fictive imagining. There is a tradition of satire which is independent of the novel and which stretches back to antiquity, and aspects of this have been important influences upon the novel. Satire attacks alleged vices and stupidities – either of individuals or of whole communities or groups – and its tools are those of ridicule, exaggeration, and contempt.

Jonathan Swift's satirical writings – and especially his *Gulliver's Travels* (1726) – are extremely important staging-posts for the novel without actually being novels themselves. If we think of Mark Twain's *The Adventures of Huckleberry Finn* (1884) we can see how the mature novel of the nineteenth century was able to incorporate important satirical techniques from earlier writers within a much more realistic framework than Swift, for example, provides. The use of a naïve narrator travelling among people whose ways are strange to him and which he describes innocently while at the same time conveying his creator's bitting satire of what they stand for is one element which unites Swift's and Twain's major works.

The satirist is by definition more concerned to draw our attention to what he or she is attacking than to create characters, situations and events that are believable in and for themselves. A novelist may however include satirical elements in works that do not, overall, merit the term 'satirical novel' (and indeed most novelists do). Thus E.M. Forster's *Howards End* is not a satirical novel, but it does include a distinctively satirical vein in its treatment of various characters. Take the following passage from the end of the first paragraph of chapter three: Mrs Munt is considering her responsibilities towards the two Schlegel sisters, Helen and Margaret:

Sooner or later the girls would enter on the process known as throwing themselves away, and if they had delayed hitherto it was only that they might throw themselves more vehemently in the future. They saw too many people at Wickham Place – unshaven musicians, an actress even, German cousins (one knows what foreigners are), acquaintances picked up at continental hotels (one knows what they are too). It was interesting, and down at Swanage no one appreciated culture more than Mrs Munt; but it was dangerous, and disaster was bound to come.

On one level this passage is a good example of *irony:* the surface meanings of the statements it contains are diametrically opposed to the underlying meanings which we attribute to narrator or author (Forster clearly does *not* believe that no-one in Swanage appreciates culture more than Mrs Munt!). But the passage is complicated by the fact that it is also satirical: it attempts to diminish a set of beliefs by making them appear ridiculous. Although the passage is ostensibly related to us from the viewpoint of Forster's narrator it mimics Mrs Munt and makes her views seem absurd by pretending to adopt them (Forster uses a technique known as Free Indirect Speech here, about which I will talk in my section 6(i) below on narrative technique).

If we compare *Howards End* with Joseph Heller's *Catch 22*

(1961) we will appreciate, I think, that the latter can more properly be termed a satirical novel than the former. Heller's dominating concern is clearly to diminish war and the military in our eyes by making them appear ridiculous and vain; his major aim in the novel is, in other words, satirical. *Howards End*, in contrast, contains satirical elements but it is not dominated by these – indeed, as the novel progresses they loom less and less large. In *Catch 22* we feel that the satire is unremitting and consistent; almost any page of the work will reveal typical examples.

The bildungsroman/erziehungsroman (novel of formation or education)

The German term Bildungsroman is now generally used in English to denote that sort of novel which concentrates upon one character's development from early youth to some sort of maturity. Goethe's *Wilhelm Meister's Apprenticeship (1795-6)*, Dickens's *David Copperfield* (1849–50), and James Joyce's *Portrait of the Artist as a Young Man* (1916) can all be described as bildungsroman.

This type of novel clearly attracts the writer interested in depicting the close relationship between early influences and later character development, and its emergence can be related to the growing interest in the theme that 'the child is father to the man' that accompanies the late eighteenth and nineteenth century interest in the young.

The roman à clef ('novel with a key')

The roman à clef is the sort of novel that can be 'unlocked' given the right 'key' – in other words one which refers to real people, places or events in disguised form so that once one realizes what the work is about the hidden references all become apparent. Thomas Love Peacock wrote several humorous novels in the early nineteenth century in which thinly disguised portrayals of such as Shelley and Coleridge appeared.

As with many of the terms under consideration here, a central question is whether a work is dominated by a particular characteristic or whether the latter plays only a minor or subservient function within it. Thus we do not call a novel a roman à clef simply because it contains one thinly disguised (or even thickly disguised) portrayal of a real person. *Sons and Lovers* (1913) is not a roman à clef because Paul Morel has a lot in common with the real D.H. Lawrence. Thomas Mann's *The Magic Mountain* (1924) was much admired by the Hungarian Marxist critic Georg Lukács, who apparently did not recognize what is allegedly the case – that the highly unpleasant character Naphta in the novel was based upon Lukács himself. Again, it would be absurd to use this claim as a reason for calling *The Magic Mountain* a roman à clef.

The Roman à thèse/tendenzroman (thesis novel)

The roman à thèse has, as the term suggests, a particular thesis or argument underlying it. It is typically a novel concerned to encourage social reform, or the correction of a particular abuse or wrong. Central to the definition is the idea of a *dominant* and usually a simple and uncomplicated thesis. Harriet Beecher Stowe's *Uncle Tom's Cabin* (1852), which is structured around an attack upon the institution of slavery in the United States is a classic roman à thèse. A novel like Thomas Hardy's *Jude The Obscure* (1896) in contrast, although it undeniably involves an attack upon certain social conventions which are seen as repressive and although in a sense it clearly 'calls for' a change in society so that women and working people have greater opportunities for self-development and for education, is too complex and involved a novel to be termed a roman à thèse. A good test is to ask whether the aim of a novel can be summed up simply as 'An attack upon "X" '; if not, then it is unwise to refer to it as a roman à thèse. As these comments suggest, the term has a pejorative ring to many ears.

The roman noir/gothic novel

The more usual term in English is 'gothic novel'. The term denotes a type of fiction that was ushered in by Horace Walpole's *The Castle of Otranto* (1764). Walpole was much influenced by the revival of interest in the Gothic that occurred in the later eighteenth century, a revival that can be seen as a precursor of aspects of Romanticism in its predilection for the wild, the uncanny, and the horrific – all of which were associated with the medieval period. The gothic novel introduced stock characters, situations and settings that still survive in the modern horror film: gloomy medieval settings, ancient castles with secret rooms and passages ruled over by a sinister nobleman tortured by a guilty secret, and a strongly supernatural element. The gothic novel proper flourished for a limited period, and is more or less a thing of the past by the early nineteenth century, but gothic elements can be found in a wide range of fiction during the nineteenth and even twentieth centuries. Jane Austen parodies aspects of the gothic novel in *Northanger Abbey* (begun in 1798 and published in 1816). The term 'gothic' has been applied to the works of Mervyn Peake much more recently, and the survival of the gothic in popular film and literature probably guarantees that it will remain a continuing influence on serious literature.

The roman-fleuve

This term denotes a series of sequence of novels which can be read and appreciated individually but which deal with recurring characters and/or common events and which form a sequence or which complement one another. Perhaps the best-known example is Balzac's *La Comedie Humaine*, but Anthony Powell's *A Dance to the Music of Time* (1951–75) is a more recent example. The roman-fleuve is closely related to what is called the *saga novel* – a series of novels about a large family each of which concentrates upon different branches of the family or different events in which it is implicated. Thomas Mann's tetralogy *Joseph and his Brothers* (1933–43) is one twentieth-century example, John Galsworthy's *Forsyte Saga* (1906-35) another.

The roman feuilleton

This is a novel that is published in installments in unabridged form by a daily newspaper. The method of publication is unusual today, but was more common in the nineteenth century.

Science fiction

Science fiction is very much a flourishing and still developing genre, and for that reason it is more difficult to define. Some definitions link it with *fantastic* literature, and the two are clearly closely related. But whereas fantasy literature normally invokes the strong possibility of supernatural agencies, science fiction need not do this. Science fiction is rather characterized by settings involving interplanetary travel, advanced technology, and is typically set in the future. In contrast to fantasy literature its settings and events are often conceivable but not actual.

Jules Verne and H.G. Wells are often granted the joint title of the father of science fiction, and its best-known practitioners today are Ray Bradbury, Arthur C. Clarke, and Isaac Asimov. Science fiction is very much an American phenomenon, although writers of other nationalities have achieved recognition in the field. There are even Soviet science fiction writers.

It is possible to relate science fiction to a work such as Swift's *Gulliver's Travels*, and clearly science fiction can have a 'pastoral' element: commenting upon one society or community under the pretext of describing another, imagined one.

The nouveau roman (new novel)

The nouveau roman is a comparatively recent development stemming from France in which the accepted conventions of fictional composition are deliberately distorted or flouted in order to disorient the reader and to achieve a different sort of effect. As such it can be seen as a recent and extreme form of *modernism* (see Chapter 5 below), and indeed a comparable group of (mainly) American novels are known as *post-modernist* novels.

The best-known French exponents of the nouveau roman are Alain Robbe-Grillet (whose book *Pour un Nouveau Roman* [1963] originated the term), Michel Butor, and Nathalie Sarraute. Prominent American post-modernists are Donald Barthelme, Ronald Sukenick, John Barth and Walter Abish.

Metafiction

Metafiction is, literally, fiction about fiction – normally denoting the sort of novel or short story which deliberately breaks fictive illusions and comments directly upon its own fictive nature or process of composition. The English father-figure of metafiction is Lawrence Sterne, in whose *Tristram Shandy* (1760–67) the narrator jokes with and teases the reader in various ways – advising him or her to turn back several pages to read a passage afresh, for example.

One of the best-known recent examples of such writing is John Fowles's *The French Lieutenant's Woman* (1969).

Faction

The term comes from the American author Truman Capote and is a portmanteau word (= fact + fiction) to refer to novels such as his own *In Cold Blood* (1966). In this work primarily novelistic techniques are used to bring actual historical events to life for the reader. The term has thus come to denote a work that is on the borderline between fact and fiction, concerned primarily with a real event or persons, but using imagined detail to increase readability and verisimilitude.

4 The Short Story and the Novella

Although length is the obvious distinguishing feature which separates the novel from the short story and the novella it is by no means the only one.

The short story is normally read at one sitting – Edgar Allan Poe in fact suggested that this was a necessary feature of the short story. Because of this the reading of a short story tends to be less reflective and more concentrated an experience; we rarely stop several times for prolonged thought in the middle of reading a short story. The short story typically limits itself to a brief span of time, and rather than showing its characters developing and maturing will show them at some revealing moment of crisis – whether internal or external. Short stories rarely have complex plots; again the focus is upon a particular episode or situation rather than a chain of events.

Thus much of the skill of the short story writer has to be devoted to making characters appear three-dimensional in spite of the fact that we see them only for a very short period of time. In addition care has to be taken to render atmosphere and situation convincingly. Very often the short story writer will use something akin to shock tactics to make the reader think and respond: an unexpected ending, a dramatic unveiling, a surprising twist of plot.

The *novella* is usually rather longer than is a short story, and although it may be read at a single sitting it most probably is usually not. Joseph Conrad's *Heart of Darkness* (first book publication 1902) can be seen as a classic novella, and any reader of this work will probably understand that the terms 'novel' and 'short story' seem somehow inappropriate to describe it. The novella has flourished far more in Germany than elsewhere, and theories of the novella are often constructed with particular reference to the German novella tradition. This apart, it does seem to be the case that the novella often has a dominant symbol or complex of symbols at its heart, and that it is these rather than the complexity of its plot that give the novella its depth and significance.

The actual story of *Heart of Darkness* could be summarized in a few lines; whatever we read this work for it is not for complexity of plot development. Instead we need to pay attention to Conrad's use of symbol and image in the work, to the complexities of narrative technique (the 'tale within a tale'), and to the texture of the prose. The novella is dominated by the 'inner narrator' Marlow's fascination with, and search for, the mysterious figure of Kurtz. Early on in the story Marlow comes across a painting that Kurtz has executed:

Then I noticed a small sketch in oils, on a panel, representing a woman, draped and blindfolded, carrying a lighted torch. The background was sombre – almost black. The movement of the woman was stately, and the effect of the torch-light on the face was sinister.

We see here, I think, how a work lacking a complicated plot can be given a complex unity through the use of other means. The picture is one of a number of symbolic 'moments' in the work which draw various threads together in a masterly way. We note a relationship between the blindfolded woman carrying a lighted torch and those Europeans (including Kurtz) who have claimed that they are bringing light to Africa but who are actually 'going at it blind', either self-deceived or dishonestly plundering. We are reminded of Kurtz's fiancée – 'the Intended' – who we meet at the end of the tale and who is as blind metaphorically as the painted woman is literally. The references to light and blackness link up with a repetitive pattern of black – white images in the work which have an intricate relationship to sets of moral judgements indicated by Conrad in indirect ways.

The short-story and novella writer, in other words, does not just produce truncated novels. These different fictional genres require a different use of the resources of the writer of prose, and they should not be read or judged in the way that we read or judge a 500-page novel.

5 Realism and Modernism

In addition to the terms discussed in the previous chapter denoting particular types of novel there are two terms which refer to something wider than a type of novel or short story that it will be as well for us to consider at this point: *realism* and *modernism*. These terms are not just used in connection with the discussion of literature or of fiction, but have an application to more widespread tendencies within the culture of (primarily) the past two centuries.

Both terms are doubly complicated by the fact that each can be used both to refer to *historical periods of literature* and also to trans-historical *types of literature* (although the term 'modernism' cannot be applied to literature written before the final years of the nineteenth century). In this respect the problems associated with the use of both terms are not dissimilar to those attached to the use of the term 'romanticism', another term which can also be used to denote both a tightly delimited period of literature and also a particular variety of literature. The use of 'romanticism' too, is also complicated by the fact that it is not just to literature that it is used to refer.

Just as not all literature written during the romantic period can be seen as romantic, so too not all modern fiction is modernist. Moreover, just as there are arguments about what does or does not characterize romanticism, so too there is by no means any universal agreement as to what constitutes realism or modernism in the novel.

Given all these complications it might be thought wise merely to avoid using either term. This simple solution is not, unfortunately, a viable one. The history of the novel is so intimately bound up with the issue of realism that we can hardly talk about the novel without addressing it. Moreover, that there is a family of new characteristics to be found in much modern art and literature can scarcely be disputed, and the term 'modernism' allows us to isolate these characteristics and to distinguish between radically different lines of development in the art and literature of the present century.

We saw in our earlier discussion of the emergence and development of the novel that the genre is distinguished by what we can call its 'formal realism' – in other words its presentation to the reader of a world that resembles our familiar, everyday world in important ways, ways not shared by the romance. The novel is stocked with people and places that *seem real* even if they are imagined, whereas the romance is peopled with people and places that seem (and were meant to seem) unreal in important ways. We can note, furthermore, that 'realism' is a term which a large number of novelists have felt the need to use in connection with discussions of the novel.

On a simple level it can be said that something – a character, an event, a setting – is 'realistic' if it resembles a model in everyday life. The matter becomes more complex, however, when we remember that a novelist can make us think seriously and critically about the real world by creating characters, events and settings that in many ways diverge from what we would expect in everyday life – in 'reality'. Think how many unusual coincidences and extraordinary events there are in those novels which are normally described as highly realistic; George Eliot's *Middlemarch* (1871/2) or Thomas Mann's *The Magic Mountain*, for example.

We have seen that the novel emerges in some sharp contrast to the romance, and is more realistic than the romance in the important sense that it directs its readers' attention towards the real world rather than offering an escape from the real world (and this is true, paradoxically, even when the actual reading of a novel can be a pleasant escape from immediate concerns and problems). But elements from the romance, as I have already suggested, can be used to explore our sense of the real: think of Swift's use of fantastic details in *Gulliver's Travels*, of James's suggestion of the supernatural in 'The Turn of the Screw' (1898), and of the use made by science fiction writers of imagined worlds.

The term 'realism' very often implies that the artist (and I repeat that this is not limited to the literary artist) has tried to include a wider and more representative coverage of social life in his or her work, and in particular that he or she has extended the coverage of the work to include 'low life' and the experiences of those deemed unworthy of artistic portrayal by other artists. The very realism of the early novel was intimately related in the public mind with the fact that it often concerned itself with the lives of the sort of human being who would not only never have entered into the romance, but whose depiction was clearly out-of-bounds for the eighteenth-century poet. Fielding's Joseph Andrews, Defoe's Moll Flanders, Smollett's Humphry Clinker – none of these characters or their real-life equivalents could have entered into the polite world of Alexander Pope. And this is one of the reasons why *Joseph Andrews* (1742), *Moll Flanders*, and *Humphry Clinker* are generally taken to be more realistic works than 'The Rape of the Lock'.

'Realism' also has a specific reference to a particular literary movement which started in France in the early nineteenth century, and flourished in the latter part of the century. The names of the novelists most associated with this movement are those of Balzac, Stendhal, and Zola. These writers made enormous efforts to ensure that 'factual details' in their works were 'correct' – that is to say, capable of being checked against an external reality by empirical investigations. They achieved this accuracy by lengthy and painstaking research. 'Realism' in connection with these writers is thus both a term denoting a group of novelists and also a term referring to a particular *method* of composition. (See also the comments on 'naturalism' below.)

The British heirs of the French realists included Arnold Bennett and George Moore – the former attacked by Virginia Woolf in essays such as 'Mr Bennett and Mrs Brown' (1924) for being a 'materialist' who was more interested in external details than in that inner life which, according to her, 'escapes' from his works.

One conclusion that can be drawn from the foregoing is that a term like 'realistic' should be used only with extreme care in connection with a novel; it is a problematic rather than a self-obvious term and raises complex questions about what 'reality' is (our fantasies are after all real in the sense that they really exist and are related to our experiences in the real world), and about the means whereby a novelist explores the real. But having said all this it remains important to be able to distinguish between novels that – in however complex and indirect a way – cause us to think about reality critically, and those which encourage us not to try but rather to escape from reality into a world of illusory imaginings.

Naturalism is a variety of realism, and the term is used in much the same way but with a narrower focus. Strictly speaking, naturalism should be restricted to a description of those literary works which were written according to a method founded upon the belief that there is a natural (rather than supernatural or spiritual) explanation for everything that exists or occurs. Naturalist novelists include the Goncourt brothers, Zola, George Moore, the German Gerhard Hauptmann, and Americans such as Theodore Dreiser and Stephen Crane.

It should be said in conclusion that although twentieth-century fiction is often divided in very broad terms into 'realist' and 'modernist' fiction, this should not be taken to imply that non-modernist fiction is somehow old-fashioned and un-modern, although it is true that many writers and critics have assumed and argued that this is the case. Moreover, the survival of realist conventions (a plot based upon cause-and-effect, well-defined characters, a general assumption that the world is knowable and susceptible to rational enquiry) in much popular fiction gives food for thought. One can posit either that the 'common reader' is old-fashioned in his or her tastes, or alternatively that those writers and readers who produce and consume modernist fiction have a different view of reality – a different world-view – from the mass of the population who read detective stories, science fiction, and popular romance.

Modernism is a term which has come into more general use only comparatively recently. It refers to those art works (or the principles behind their creation) produced since the end of the nineteenth century which decisively reject the artistic conventions of the previous age. Foremost among such rejected conventions are those associated with realism. In particular, modernist works tend to be *self-conscious* in ways that vary according to the genre or art-form in question; they deliberately remind the reader or observer that they *are* art-works, rather than seeking to serve as 'windows on reality'. Whereas one may forget that one is reading a novel when immersed in, say, *War and Peace* (1865–68) – responding to characters and events as if they were 'real' – this is something of which one is constantly reminded when reading a modernist work such as Virginia Woolf's *The Waves* (1931). Thus Picasso's rejection of representational art and of the conventions of perspective in his early paintings can be compared with the rejection of the 'tyranny of plot' by novelists such as Joyce, Woolf, and the Frenchman Marcel Proust. A good example of this shift in attitudes from realism to modernism can be found in the novels and other writings of Joseph Conrad, who in many ways represents a transitional figure between realist and modernist conventions. In 1898 Conrad wrote to a friend, 'You must have a *plot*! If you haven't, every fool reviewer will kick you because there can't be literature without plot.' And four years later, in 1902, he wrote to Arnold Bennett (one of Woolf's 'materialists' and thus far from what we now call modernism), 'You stop just short of being absolutely real because you are faithful to your dogmas of realism. Now realism in art will never approach reality.'[7]

What we see here is 'the tide on the turn'; a writer – representative of many other writers and artists – beginning to question 'dogmas of realism' and to search for alternatives: alternatives to the well-made plot, the rounded and lifelike character, the knowable world wholly accessible to reasoned and rational enquiry.

The modernist novel typically focuses far greater attention on to the states and processes *inside* the consciousness of the main character(s) than on to public events in the outside world. If the twentieth century is the century of Freud and Marx then we can say that the modernist novel has much more in common with the former than the latter (which explains, incidentally, why an orthodox Marxist critic such as the Hungarian Georg Lukács argued so bitterly for realism and against modernism during his long life).

This focusing upon the inner life has encouraged the development of new *methods* of fictional expression. If modernism can be defined negatively in terms of its rejection of realist conventions and assumptions, its positive side can be seen in its remarkable development of techniques such as *stream of consciousness* and *internal monologue*, and revolutions in the use of poetic expression in the novel. More will be said about such techniques in my next chapter.

A brief comment should be added concerning the philosophical underpinnings of modernism. These are very often implicit rather than overt, but frequently we find that modernist novels are pessimistic in tone, unsure about the sense or logic of the world, and look on human beings as isolated and alienated. The philosophical corollary of the rejection of perspective in art, and of an omniscient view of a knowable world obeying certain laws in fiction, seems to be a view of reality as lacking any unifying logic; different perspectives have to be combined because although they may be contradictory there is no way of deciding between them. These are generalizations of course, and generalizations are always dangerous, but they are worth bearing in mind when reading novels by Franz Kafka, Virginia Woolf, and other modernists.

6 Analysing Fiction

(i) Narrative technique

In my opening chapter I drew attention to the fact that everything we read in a novel comes to us via some sort of 'telling'. We are told what happens in a novel; no matter how successful the novelist is in making a scene seem dramatic it is never dramatic in the way that a play or a film is. We may feel that we 'see', but we see as a result of what we visualize in response to a narrative not an enactment.

However in one respect the writing of a novel is comparable to the making of a film. When we watch a film we seem to be seeing 'things as they are'; 'reality'. But a director has *chosen how* we see these things, this reality; he or she has decided whether the camera will be placed high or low, whether there will be rapid cuts from one camera angle to another or not, whether a camera will follow one character as he or she walks along a street – and so on. One scene in a film could be shot innumerable ways, and each of these ways would produce a different effect upon the audience. Even with a simple conversation between two characters the audience's attitude towards each character can be affected by different camera angles, cutting, and so on. (Anyone who has played around with a video camera will quickly have discovered this.)

The novelist has a far greater range of choices open to him or her than does the film director. Let us go through some of the most important of these choices.

To start with, the author can have the story told through the mediation of a *personified narrator*, a 'teller' who the reader recognizes as a distinct person with defined individual human characteristics, or alternatively the narrative source can seem so undefined as to make it doubtful whether or not we are dealing with an individualized human source. Thus the narrator of Sterne's *Tristram Shandy* has a distinct personality which is thrust at us in the opening words of the novel:

I wish either my father or my mother, or indeed both of them, as they were in duty both equally bound to it, had minded what they were about when they begot me . . .

The opening of D.H. Lawrence's *Sons and Lovers* (1913), in contrast, strikes us as far more impersonal; whereas the opening of Sterne's novel draws our attention to the narrator, who is talking about himself, the narrative of *Sons and Lovers* focuses our attention on to what is told rather than who tells or how:

'The Bottoms' succeeded to 'Hell Row'. Hell Row was a block of thatched, bulging cottages that stood by the brookside on Greenhill Lane. There lived the colliers who worked in the little gin-pits two fields away.

Some narrators may even have names and detailed personal histories, as does Nick Carraway, the narrator of F. Scott Fitzgerald's *The Great Gatsby* (1925). Other narrators may just indicate to us that they are persons – perhaps by the occasional use of 'I' in their narrative – but will tell us no more about themselves than this. In Henry James's *The Turn of the Screw* for example we have a complex narrative structure; an unnamed, 'outer' narrator reports on a scene during which another character named Douglas undertakes to read a story told to him years before by an unnamed governess of his, a written copy of which he has been given by her. The outer narrator then describes Douglas's introductory comments and gives us some comments upon his reading of the manuscript, but reproduces that manuscript for the benefit of readers.

(It is interesting to note that many readers and critics assume that the outer narrator is a man – perhaps because 'he' makes many dismissive remarks about the ladies present – but there is no direct evidence that this is the case. Christine Brooke-Rose, in her book *A Rhetoric of the Unreal* [1981] takes many critics of *The Turn of the Screw* to task for reading details in to the work that are not there, but she herself refers to the outer narrator as 'he'. The example shows how *active* the reader inevitably is in creating an image of a narrator on the basis of hints and suggestions in the text. A skilled author will, of course, make use of this fact.)

We have a similar combination of an outer, unnamed narrator and a named 'inner' narrator in Joseph Conrad's *Heart of Darkness*, although here we have no written document that is reproduced, but rather the tale told to a small group by Marlow (the 'inner' narrator) is given to the reader via the anonymous outer narrator.

There is much that can be said about both James's and Conrad's narrative technique, but for the time being I would like to comment upon the fact that both feel the need for a combination of named and unnamed narrators. The granting of a name probably intensifies the degree of personification, the extent to which we think of a narrative source as human and individual, although some unnamed narrators (Jane Austen's, for example) can appear to the reader as highly individual and possessed of something like a personality. (Or is it, rather, that we have a detailed knowledge of the values and attitudes relating to Jane Austen's narratives, without necessarily individualizing or personifying them?)

If we turn to Charles Dickens's novel *Bleak House* (1852–3), and focus upon those parts of it which are not told by the personified narrator Esther Summerson, we see something very different. Chapter 20 opens thus:

The long vacation saunters on towards term-time, like an idle river very leisurely strolling down a flat country to the sea. Mr Guppy saunters along with it congenially. He has blunted the blade of his pen-knife, and broken the point off, by sticking that instrument into his desk in every direction. Not that he bears the desk any ill will, but he must do something . . .

This narrative seems human perhaps in its gentle irony, but its viewpoint corresponds to no possible human viewpoint in ordinary life. The narrator is uninvolved dramatically in the scene, but he (is it he?) knows what is going on in Mr Guppy's head – perhaps better than does Mr Guppy. Yet at other points in this narrative the narrator betrays an ignorance of things that we have learned from Esther Summerson's narrative. (So the narrator certainly cannot be Charles Dickens himself!)

It is worth noting Dickens's use of the present tense in this extract; the anonymous narrator of *Bleak House* frequently uses this tense, and it has a very definite effect on the way the reader responds to the narrative. We often use the present tense to tell stories or jokes, and so one effect of Dickens's use of this tense here is to make the narrative seem more familiar, intimate, colloquial. At the same time, the use of the present tense gives the scene more *dramatic* force: we feel that we are actually watching Mr Guppy as he is doing something, not via the recollection of a narrator. The main point I want to make here, however, is that although there are situations outside of literature in which we deliver present-tense narratives, the extract I have quoted could be nothing other than literary. If we suddenly turned the radio on and heard these words being read, or if we discovered them on a scrap of paper somewhere, we would still know that they had to come from a piece of fiction, for in no other situation would this content and this narrative style be found in such combination.

In addition to choosing a narrator or narrative source, the novelist can (but need not) select a stated or implied *medium* for his or her narrative. Now of course all novels consist of printed words in a literal sense, but a novel may well be presented to the reader as if it were spoken rather than written, or thought, or it may even be presented in such a way as to suggest that it is a sort of medium-less narrative – something impossible outside the realms of literature.

Thus to take two very different examples, Agatha Christie's *The Murder of Roger Ackroyd* (1926) and Feodor Dostoyevsky's *Notes from Underground* (1864) are both presented to the reader as *written* documents. We learn this only towards the end of Christie's story, when the narrator explains the circumstances of his writing his account (and that should make us pause for thought: think of the oddness of reading a story and not knowing until the end of the story whether it is a written document we are reading: that is because the written text *we* see stands for another text, about the precise nature of which we can be left in the dark by the novelist). In Dostoyevsky's story we find the following interpolated comment on the first page:

(A poor witticism; but I won't cross it out. When I wrote that down, I thought it would seem very pointed: now, when I see that I was simply trying to be clever and cynical, I shall leave it in on purpose.)

We may well ask: why should one author want to reveal the implied narrative medium of the story on the first page, and another only towards the end? What difference does it make to the reader's response to the story?

Where a novelist does not state his or her implied narrative medium, all sorts of variations are possible. Emily Brontë's *Wuthering Heights* opens as if it might be some sort of diary entry:

1801. – I have just returned from a visit to my landlord – the solitary neighbour that I shall be troubled with. This is certainly a beautiful country!

But other parts of the novel, also told by Mr Lockwood as is this opening passage, read more like thought-processes than writing. This is the third paragraph of chapter 10:

This is quite an easy interval. I am too weak to read, yet I feel as if I could enjoy something interesting. Why not have up Mrs Dean to finish her tale? I can recollect its chief incidents, as far as she had gone. Yes, I remember her hero had run off, and never been heard of for three years: and the heroine was married: I'll ring; she'll be delighted to find me capable of talking cheerfully.
Mrs Dean came.

Some narratives can be entirely unspecific. Joseph Conrad's *The Shadow-Line* (1916–17), for example, could be written, spoken or thought in origin; it is indeed probably wrong to try to fix a medium for it as it represents a sort of medium-less, pure narrative which we take in as readers without worrying about its physical origin.

Closely related to the foregoing issues is that of *language*. Whether a narrative is formal or colloquial, for example, depends a lot upon whether it is told by a personified or unpersonified narrator, and upon whether we are to assume that it is spoken, written, or thought. (Conversely, of course, the degree of formality of a novel's language may lead us to infer that a narrative is, for example, a spoken tale by a personified narrator.) Language in one sense is the medium of a novel as paint is the medium of a painting, but this is a very bad comparison in general as painters do not represent paint whereas novelists *do* often represent language: *Heart of*

Darkness, for example, is not just *in* language, it *represents language* – the language uttered by Marlow. Thus in one sense the *actual* medium of this novel – language – is also its *implied* medium. But whilst a novel's actual medium is written language its implied medium need not be, and indeed as I have already pointed out a novel need have no implied medium at all, and the text of a novel need not even represent language, it could represent a state of mind, a sequence of events and experiences that have not necessarily been verbalized by anyone but which are translated into words for the reader by the novelist.

Let us pause for a moment and ask why all this is important. What difference does it make? Well, in everyday life *who* tells us a story, and *how* make a very big difference. The statement that the economy has never been stronger has a different effect on us if told by the Prime Minister from the effect it has on us if we read it in an opposition newspaper. A proposal of marriage uttered directly, in emotional speech, strikes the recipient rather differently from one formally written and received by post. Source and medium affect the *selection*, the *authority*, and the *attitude towards what is recounted* of the narrative – and thus, of course, the effect on the reader or listener. And the same is true with the novel: different narrators, different narrative media *change* a story, they affect not just how we are told something but what we are told, and what attitude we take towards what we are told.

Nobody knows this better than novelists themselves, and there are some fascinating accounts by different novelists of the problematic process that deciding upon a narrative technique involves. The recently published volume of letters by Jean Rhys includes a number of letters which provide relevant evidence concerning her choice of narrative perspective for her novel *Wide Sargasso Sea* (1966). To her daughter, in 1959, Jean Rhys writes about the forthcoming novel:

It can be done 3 ways. (1) Straight. Childhood. Marriage, Finale told in 1st person. Or it can be done (2) Man's point of view (3) Woman's ditto both 1st person. Or it can be told in the third person with the writer as the Almighty. . . .
   I am doing (2).[8]

Later on in the same year Jean Rhys wrote to Francis

Wyndham admitting that the novel had already been written three times, first told by the heroine in the first person, second told by the housekeeper Mrs Poole as the 'I', and now using two 'I's: 'Mr Rochester and his first wife'. (The novel is based on and closely related to Charlotte Brontë's *Jane Eyre* [1847]). According to Rhys it was unsatisfactory to have the heroine tell all the story herself because the result was obscure and 'all on one note', and it was also unsatisfactory to have the house-keeper Grace Poole tell the whole story because although tech-nically this was the best solution the character 'wouldn't come to life'.[9]

So we can see that it can be a matter of trial and error for a novelist to hit on the right narrative perspective.

Other considerations can also be important. Christopher Isherwood's autobiography *Christopher and his Kind* contains an enthralling account of his problems in fixing the narrative perspective of his novel *Mr Norris Changes Trains* (1935). He felt that he wanted the reader to experience Arthur Norris personally, and believed that this could only be done by writing in the first person, subjectively, and having the nar-rator meet Norris. But the narrator could not be Christopher Isherwood because Isherwood was not prepared to reveal his own homosexuality publicly by having the narrator an avowed homosexual, although he scorned to have the nar-rator heterosexual. Thus the narrator of the work ends up with no explicit sex-experiences in the story, and was dubbed a 'sexless nitwit' by one reviewer. But an additional interesting aspect of the problem is mentioned by Isherwood. He wanted the reader's attention to be concentrated upon Norris and not on the narrator, and if the narrator had been made a homo-sexual he would have become so 'odd' and interesting that he would have thrown the novel out of balance by attracting too much of the reader's attention.

Isherwood makes a further interesting point. He notes that if a narrator is given no personal qualities then when something happens to him the reader will assume that his responses are not likely to be unusual; the reader can thus identify with the narrator and experience with and through him. But a narrator who is somehow 'odd' will prevent the reader from identifying with him even if he or she is sympathetic to him.[10]

Let us return to the issue of narrative choice in the light of our understanding of the crucial importance of such decisions by the novelist. Many critics have found it useful to distinguish between *reliable* and *unreliable* narrators, a distinction that touches upon some of the points raised by Isherwood. We can also note that reliability apart, we associate some narrative perspectives more with the views and position of actual authors, and some not at all (or far less) with their creators. In general we can say that a single, consistent, unpersonified voice is more likely to be associated with authorial beliefs than a personified narrator in a novel with many narrators – although of course in both cases this depends upon the attitudes expressed in and revealed by the narrative.

Thus it is easier to assume that the opinions expressed by the anonymous narrator of Conrad's *The Shadow-Line* are close to those of Conrad himself than it is in the case of his personified narrator Marlow, who appears in a number of his works. Moreover, even if Marlow is a generally reliable narator, we do not take everything he says on quite the same trust as we do what we learn from the narrator of *The Shadow-Line*, simply because we see Marlow from the outside and treat him as another person, whereas we experience with the narrator of *The Shadow-Line* and, as we read, think ourselves fully into his position from the inside.

Consistency is a crucial issue here. An inconsistent narrator cannot be wholly reliable by his or her own testimony. The fact that Swift's Gulliver in his *Gulliver's Travels* seems to vary from book to book, being alternatively percipient and obtuse, blindly patriotic and unchauvinistically humanistic, warns us that we can relax into no consistent attitude to his actions or opinions. On the other hand, although few if any readers of *Wuthering Heights* can identify totally with Mr Lockwood he is consistently portrayed, and so we feel more and more confident at assessing his opinions in the light of our view of his personality and character.

In addition to choosing a narrator and (perhaps) an implied narrative medium, the novelist has to select a *form of address* for his narrator. The narrative can, for instance, be directly addressed to 'the reader' ('Dear Reader . . .'), or it can be spoken or written as it were into a void. In his novel *Tom Jones* Henry Fielding uses 'interchapters' in which the reader is addressed directly, while the remainder of the novel is less overtly pointed at any reader or listener. What do we make of the opening lines of Albert Camus's *The Outsider* (1942)?

Mother died today. Or, maybe, yesterday; I can't be sure. The tele-
gram from the Home says: *Your mother passed away. Funeral
tomorrow. Deep sympathy.* Which leaves the matter doubtful; it could
have been yesterday.

Clearly this could be addressed to someone (would there be
any sense in saying it to oneself?), but the narrative might
represent a state of mind and a sequence of events which the
reader is not meant to think are actually aimed at any recipient
in particular.

Narratives can also involve such elements as *complicity,
intrusion,* and *intimacy* – things instantly recognized by
readers but often tricky to analyse.

Take for example the following brief extract from chapter
three of E.M. Forster's *Howards End*, in which Mrs Munt is
talking at cross-purposes to Charles Wilcox, believing him to
be engaged to her niece Helen:

'This is very good of you,' said Mrs Munt, as she settled into a luxurious
cavern of red leather, and suffered her person to be padded with rugs
and shawls. She was more civil than she had intended, but really this
young man was very kind. Moreover, she was a little afraid of him: his
self-possession was extraordinary. 'Very good indeed,' she repeated,
adding: 'It is just what I should have wished.'

'Very good of you to say so,' he replied, with a slight look of surprise, which, like most slight looks, escaped Mrs Munt's attention.

That final narrative comment is the culminating stroke in a
process whereby the reader is sucked into complicity with the
narrator. We are amused with the narrator at Mrs Munt's
obtuseness and self-importance, and as a result of such passages we are likely to be far more malleable in the hands of the
narrator, far more willing to accept his value-judgements and
assessments of characters.

If we think of Jane Austen's intimate address to the reader in
her novels, and Henry Fielding's intrusive interpolation of
interchapters in *Tom Jones* we can see that the narrator has a
wide variety of relationships with the narrated events and
characters, and with the reader, at his or her disposal.
Choosing the right relationships is at the heart of success as a
writer of fiction. For many readers, the last paragraph of
Thomas Hardy's *Tess of the d'Urbervilles* (1891) starts with an

annoyingly intrusive and heavy-handed narrator comment, a comment which such readers feel detracts from the power of the scene depicted at this point of the novel. In contrast, at the end of the first chapter of Jane Austen's *Mansfield Park* we find this concluding sentence about Mrs Price (Fanny's mother): 'Poor woman! she probably thought change of air might agree with many of her children.' Although technically intrusive, this seems less to break in upon an established tone or perspective than does Hardy's comment, and so seems to have offended fewer readers than has that final paragraph of *Tess of the d'Urbervilles*.

The narrator, if personified, can have a range of different sorts of relationship with the actions and events described in a novel. He or she may be an 'intradiegetic narrator' – an actor with a full part to play in the story told, or an observer of events in which he or she is personally uninvolved, or an 'extradiegetic narrator' – merely a narrator, telling a story but indicating no personal involvement in or relationship to this story, which may even be presumed to take place on another level of reality from that in which he or she exists.

In Joseph Conrad's *Heart of Darkness*, for instance, his narrator Marlow tells a story in which he personally has been involved. The 'outer', unnamed narrator in this same novella is also in a sense involved in the outer action (the 'frame') of the story, but clearly this narrator's relationship to events in the work is very different from Marlow's. In Charles Dickens's *Great Expectations* (1860–61) the narrator Pip is telling us his life story, but the great difference of age and maturity between the narrating and the narrated Pip means that the narrator can be either very involved or relatively uninvolved in the story at different times.

In *Wuthering Heights* Mr Lockwood is in a sense involved in present-time events in the novel (and the novel's time sequence is complicated enough to give us a number of different 'present times'), but he is really an observer of the key events in the work which are narrated by Nelly Dean to him. And, finally, the authorial narrator of the interchapters in Henry Fielding's *Tom Jones* exists on a different plane from the characters and events in the rest of the story, the fictive nature of which he comments upon directly.

Furthermore, we should note that a narrative can be either *recollective* or *dramatic*. Of course, *any* narrative involves recollection; to be told a story is to be informed of something which has already happened, something which is being remembered, *re*counted. But as the comment on his epistolary technique that I quoted earlier from Richardson's *Clarissa* demonstrated, some ways of telling a story can have far more dramatic effect than others. Note how Jean Rhys changes the tense used in the following passage in order to create dramatic immediacy in her novel *Good Morning, Midnight* (1939).

The lavatory at the station – that was the next time I cried. I had just been sick. I was so afraid I might be going to have a baby. . . .
Although I have been so sick, I don't feel any better. I lean up against the wall, icy cold and sweating. Someone tries the door, and I pull myself together, stop crying and powder my face.[11] (Ellipsis in original)

We can sum up much of the force of the discussion so far in this section with the question: 'What does the narrative know?' Literary critics have traditionally used the technical term *point of view* to pinpoint this particular issue. The term has the disadvantage that different critics have used it in slightly different ways, to mean either the *narrator's* relation to the story told or the *writer's* attitude to his or her work. This distinction should be borne in mind, but one should also remember of course that an author conveys something about his or her attitude towards the work by choosing a particular narrative perspective.

It is worth asking, for example, whether the narrative perspective chosen is recognizably a human one: in other words does it resemble the perspective that a real human being might have on actual characters and events? In the case of Conrad's Marlow, Defoe's Moll Flanders, Dickens's Pip or Jean Rhys's Sasha Jensen we can say that a real human being might share such a perspective on events as they have (which is not to say that such a real human being would have *told* his or her story as they do – or even at all). But no human being in real life would know what the narrator of George Eliot's *Middlemarch* (1871–72) knows about the characters and events in that work.

What difference does this make? Well, a good way to demonstrate this is by means of what we can call the *transposition test*: transposing a novel (in one's imagination) from one narrative perspective to another. Imagine *Middlemarch* told in the first person by Dorothea, or by Dorothea and Lydgate in successive sections. What would *Wuthering Heights* be like as an epistolary novel? Or told exclusively through Heathcliff's eyes? Rewriting a whole novel in such a way would be unthinkably tedious, but it can be an extremely revealing exercise to take a brief passage from a novel and to rewrite it in this manner.

It is interesting to know that Franz Kafka started his novel *The Castle* (1926) in the first person, and the manuscript of the novel has 'I', crossed out and replaced by 'K', throughout the early part of the work. If you have read this work you will appreciate how very differently it reads with 'I' rather than 'K'; the reader's whole relationship with the main character is quite different. Finding the right narrative perspective seems to have been something that Kafka achieved only after having started writing the work – when he could perhaps more easily put himself into the position of a potential reader.

Sometimes attempts to dramatize novels have the effect of demonstrating how crucial their particular narrative perspective is. Joseph Conrad attempted dramatizations of a number of his works, all of which were more or less disastrous. I think that we can easily understand that a dramatization of *The Secret Agent* (1907) (which Conrad actually completed) *would* be disastrous because it necessarily loses what is at the heart of the work's power: the bitter but pityingly ironic attitude of the narrator towards the characters and events of the novel.

For the purpose of clear exposition I have written so far much as if all novels have one, consistent, narrative perspective. But this is clearly untrue. Again we can make a useful comparison with the cinema. Early films involved one camera mounted rigidly in front of the actors like a theatre audience, before which acting took place. But before long film-makers realized that different cameras could be used and shots from each spliced together to make the film more alive – and cameras could move with the actors and could utilize long-range and close-up lenses. In this respect a sophisticated novel like *Wuthering Heights* is like a modern film: no longer do we have the single camera of novels like *Clarissa* and *Robinson Crusoe* (1719), but a range of different, moving recorders. Sometimes such shifts are almost imperceptible. Most readers need to have it pointed out to them after an initial reading of Joseph Conrad's *The Nigger of the 'Narcissus'* that although we appear to have a consistent narrative viewpoint in the work, at times the narrator seems omniscient and at times he describes himself as a crew member of the ship. Much the same is true of the narrator of Dostoyevsky's *The Devils* (1870).

It is, in conclusion, important to be able to see narrative techniques in their historical context and development, as well as appreciating the 'internal', technical reasons for developments in narrative technique. Thus we can say that the rise of the epistolary novel in the eighteenth century cannot be understood apart from the much greater importance of letter-writing at that time, and that the emergence of the stream of consciousness novel in the twentieth century has to be related to the development of modern psychology and the increasing interest in mental operations that accompanies it. The following factors are all important in assessing the significance of a particular narrative technique:

1 Changes in the dominant modes of human communication (think of the enormous effect that the telephone has had on us).
2 The effect of different world-views, philosophies, ideologies (there is clearly a parallel between a belief in a God who sees everything, and novelists' use of omniscient narrators).
3 Changes in readership patterns and habits (it is perhaps harder to feel intimate with a larger, more amorphous and anonymous set of readers – or to feel at ease with readers mainly of the opposite sex from oneself).
4 Larger changes in human life and modes of consciousness (think of the growth of urban living, of mass communication, of modern science and politics).

Let me at this point say a few words about *stream of consciousness* technique and the *internal monologue*. The two need carefully to be distinguished. An internal monologue necessarily implies the use of *language*, and if an individual is 'talking to himself or herself' then that in turn presupposes a certain amount of consciousness of what is going on in that person's mind. The famous closing section of James Joyce's *Ulysses* (1914–22) gives us, essentially, Molly Bloom's internal monologue; she is thinking to herself in words and is conscious of what she is thinking. But compare the following passage from the same novel, which concerns the character Leopold Bloom:

He stood up. Hello. Were those two buttons of my waistcoat open all the time. Women enjoy it. Annoyed if you don't. Why didn't you tell me before. Never tell you. But we. Excuse, miss, there's a (whh!) just a (whh!) fluff.[12]

This clearly follows Bloom's stream of consciousness (the term comes originally from William James, brother to Henry). But it is not absolutely clear that the words we read here represent words that Bloom himself is meant to have produced, they may, rather, be words that the narrator uses to represent unverbalized mental processes in Bloom.

This difficulty in distinguishing between what a narrator says and what a character thinks or verbalizes may become particularly acute with the use of a technique which is known by a number of different terms: 'Free Indirect Speech', 'Represented Speech (or Thought)', 'Narrated Monologue', or the German and French terms, 'Erlebte Rede' and 'Style Indirect Libre'. The complications of terminology are worth wading through, for the technique itself is arguably one of the most important in the novel since Jane Austen. Take the following passage from Katherine Mansfield's short story 'The Voyage' (1922):

'How long am I going to stay?' she whispered anxiously. He wouldn't look at her. He shook her off gently, and gently said, 'We'll see about that. Here! Where's your hand?' He pressed something into her palm. 'Here's a shilling in case you should need it.'
A shilling! She must be going away for ever! 'Father!' cried Fenella.

The part of this passage I want to draw attention to is 'A shilling! She must be going away for ever!' Now you will note that these two utterances are ostensibly in the third person; Fenella is described as 'she' and inverted commas are not used. But it is clear that it is Fenella's thoughts that are being given us here as neither the narrator nor her father would be so surprised at her being given a shilling. Free Indirect Speech involves the mixing of the characteristics of Direct and Indirect speech (in this case the use of 'she' alongside the exclamation mark normally associated with Direct Speech – it is Fenella and not the narrator who is surprised) so as to give us a character's speech or thoughts *without necessarily giving them to us in the words supposed to have been used by the character*. As I have said, the technique is extremely important in the modern novel or short story, and gives the fiction writer an enormously flexible tool to mix or alternate narrator perspective and stream of character consciousness in an unobtrusive way.

As I have also said, the technique sometimes makes it impossible definitively to attribute a statement either to narrator or character. Take this extract from Virginia Woolf's *Mrs Dalloway* (1925):

> Elizabeth rather wondered whether Miss Kilman could be hungry. It was her way of eating, eating with intensity, then looking, again and again, at a plate of sugared cakes on the table next them; then, when a lady and a child sat down and the child took the cake, could Miss Kilman really mind it? Yes, Miss Kilman did mind it. She had wanted that cake – the pink one. The pleasure of eating was almost the only pure pleasure left her, and then to be baffled even in that!

Whose consciousness is represented in the last three sentences? Is it (i) Narrator (ii) Narrator (iii) Narrator? Or (i) Narrator (ii) Narrator (iii) Miss Kilman? Or (i) Narrator (ii) Miss Kilman (iii) Miss Kilman? The fact is that the indeterminacy here is not a flaw on the passage but quite the reverse: we know what Miss Kilman is thinking and we know what the narrator's attitude towards her and her desires is without having to attribute a form of words either to the narrator or to the character.

Before we leave the topic of narrative technique, some further important terms need to be mentioned. All of these have come from relatively recent narrative theorists, and all have the disadvantage that they are terms which have alternative meanings both within literary criticism and in ordinary discourse. But even if you decide to try to do without the terms themselves, the *issues* that they point to are very important, and are worth devoting some thought to.

Firstly, *tense, tone*, and *mood*. By *tense* is meant the relationship between narrated and narrating time. A novelist can spend fifty pages to tell us about one day in the life of a heroine, and then ten further pages to cover fifty years. Within a single novel the ratio of narrated to narrating time can alter very substantially, and it is worth paying careful attention to such shifts. In *Tristram Shandy* Lawrence Sterne makes lots of jokes about the relationship between narrated and narrating time: at the start of chapter 21 for example the text breaks off into a digression in the middle of a sentence uttered by uncle Toby, to utter which he has had to take his pipe out of his mouth. The digression finished, the text continues: 'But I forget my uncle Toby, whom all this while we have left knocking the ashes out of his tobacco pipe.' The suggestion that narrated and narrating time are coterminous *is* a joke, we know, because in many novels the narrator can leap over enormous gaps of time. Think how few pages are devoted to the period of Cathy's married life prior to the return of Heathcliff in *Wuthering Heights*.

By *tone* is meant the attitude of the narrator (and sometimes, by implication, of the author) towards what is narrated. One fails to understand *Gulliver's Travels*, for example, if one does not perceive the satirical tone that pervades the whole work. And although it is true that a work like Kafka's *The Castle* suggests that life is meaningless and that communication between human beings is impossible, this aspect of the work has to be seen in consort with the tone of deep pity and sympathy for humanity which pervades the novel.

And by *mood* is meant the type of discourse used by the narrator – the sort of issue we considered earlier in connection with discussion of the term 'point of view'. The term is taken from Continental narrative theorists and is perhaps less confusing when rendered by the word 'mode', as 'mood' has other meanings even within literary criticism. We can sum up what is meant by mood/mode by saying that it refers to the *relationship* between the narrating and what is narrated in a broad sense – both in terms of *what* is perceived and reported, and in terms of *how* what is perceived and reported is treated.

Secondly, two further terms can be of particular use in the analysis of narrative technique: *voice* and *perspective*. We can sum up what these terms cover in two questions: 'Who speaks?' and 'Who sees?' In Katherine Mansfield's 'The Voyage', for instance, the voice is essentially that of a third-person narrator who is semi-omniscient and 'out of the story'. But the reader is, nevertheless, encouraged to see everything through Fenella's eyes, to experience through her senses. In this short story, then, the *voice* is that of a semi-omniscient third-person narrator, but the *perspective* is Fenella's.

If these terms have confused you don't worry; some of them may become clearer once the sections following on 'Structure' and 'Plot' have been read. And the important thing is not to learn a complicated set of terms, but to become alive to the sort of distinctions the terms point to. Thus it is a useful exercise to take a passage from a novel and then to go through it asking what there is to be said about tense, tone, mood, voice and perspective in it – for all of these terms help us to isolate particular aspects of narrative technique that are very important.

(ii) Character

'Character' may well seem to be one of the least problematic terms with which you have to deal in studying the novel. The proper names we come across in a novel – Tom Jones, Anna Karenina, Daisy Miller, Huck Finn, Yossarian – seem very much like the proper names we meet in everyday life with which we designate individual human beings.

And yet even if we stop at names we may realize that characters in novels aren't quite like real people. In everyday life we sometimes meet a person with an unusually appropriate name: the very tall person called Long or the radio engineer called Sparks. But the peculiar appropriateness of Heathcliff's name, for instance, is surely hardly ever met with in real life. And what about Dickens's Esther Summerson – who acts like a 'Summer sun' In *Bleak House*, dispelling the shadows with which the work is, initially, filled? Even 'Tom Jones' seems extraordinarily appropriate a name for the non-aristocratic, normally healthy hero of Fielding's novel given its resolute *lack* of connotations or associations.

'Tom Jones' is a rather different name from 'M'Choakunchild' – the name given by Dickens to one of his characters – however, and this reminds us of an important point: there are different *sorts* of literary character. Of course there are different sorts of people in ordinary life, but it is not this sort of variation that I have in mind. Think of Meursault in Albert Camus's *The Outsider* and Mr Guppy in Charles Dickens's *Bleak House*. Both are young men with problems of communication and an odd relation to their mothers. But there are also important differences between them, and if we were asked to explain these differences we would have to talk not just about their differences as individuals but also as characters, as literary constructions within very different sorts of novel. We could not transplant Mr Guppy to *The Outsider*; he could not survive in that novel as we know him in *Bleak House*.

Let us try to explore some of the differences that exist between literary characters. We have some well-established terms to draw on initially: major and minor characters, flat and round characters, stock characters, 'types', caricatures, and so on.

We can sum up one important distinction that has a bearing upon all of the above terms: is the writer interested in developing a character so as to *represent something*, or in order to present a *particular individuality?* The distinction is related to that between novels of 'life' and novels of 'pattern' to which I referred much earlier, for it is in novels of pattern that one is likely to find characters who stand for something (a giveaway feature is often the names) and in the novel of life that one finds characters possessed of a distinctive and idiosyncratic individuality. However, even in the latter case we have to face the paradox that a highly individualized character may also stand for something: Dickens's Mr Toots in *Dombey and Son* (1846–48) and Dostoyevsky's Prince Myshkin in *The Idiot* (1869) are 'originals', yet they also stand for certain important qualities which contribute importantly to the themes of the two novels mentioned. Moreover, just because a character is a recognizable *type* (another of Dickens's grotesques, one of Dostoyevsky's eccentrics) does not mean that he or she cannot also be a realized individual personality in the work.

Some characters seem far more independent of their history and surroundings than is normally the case in real life. In his book *Aspects of the Novel* (1927) E.M. Forster uses Dickens's Mrs Micawber (from *David Copperfield*) as an example of what he calls a 'flat character':

The really flat character can be expressed in one sentence such as 'I never will desert Mr Micawber.' There is Mrs Micawber – she says she won't desert Mr Micawber; she doesn't, and there she is.

In real life this sort of independence of events surely does not exist. Mrs Micawber does not change because she is not allowed to *interact* with other people and situations; she is independent of them.

A novelist may use a character for purposes quite other than characterization. A character may do 'uncharacteristic' things in order to further the plot for the author; a character may be associated with actions or objects for a purpose connected with the theme of the novel; a character may say things just so that the reader can be told something.

To say that there are different types of character is to say in effect that novelists use characters and character portrayals for a range of different purposes. This is why it is a mistake always to talk about characters in a novel as if they were real people; clearly the novelist relies upon our knowledge of and reactions to real people in his or her creation of character, but characters are often created by novelists for purposes other than that of investigation into human personality or psychology. They can be used to tell a story, to exemplify a belief, to contribute to a symbolic pattern in a novel, or merely to facilitate a particular plot development.

Moreover, novelists can create character in a range of different ways. A classic but still useful distinction between two fundamental ways of creating (or 'revealing') character is that which we owe to Percy Lubbock's *The Craft of Fiction* (1921). Lubbock's distinction between 'telling' and 'showing' (a distinction he probably owed to Henry James) is very similar to that which the Hungarian Marxist critic Georg Lukács makes between 'narration' and 'description' in a famous essay entitled 'Narrate or Describe' (1936). (In neither case, it should be said, is the critic talking exclusively about characterization.) When Jane Austen opens her novel *Emma* (1816) in the following way she is *telling* (or in Lukács's terminology describing) rather than showing us what Emma is like:

Emma Woodhouse, handsome, clever, and rich, with a comfortable home and happy disposition, seemed to unite some of the best blessings of existence; and had lived nearly twenty-one years in the world with very little to distress or vex her.

But when, later on in the novel, we witness the conversation between Emma and Mr Knightley in which he criticizes her rudeness to Miss Bates we are *shown* the sort of person Emma is through her behaviour and her responses to him. Since Lubbock, critics have generally preferred 'showing' to 'telling' as a method of revealing character, feeling that this method unlocks the life in characters rather than treating them (as Lukács puts it) as inanimate objects. Moreover we feel that *we* decide what a character is like when we observe him or her behaving in front of us, we can use our critical intelligence and our knowledge of human beings to reach an assessment of them. Whereas when we are told something we can only take it or leave it. There is no scope for differential responses to the first sentence of *Emma*. (This is why, in real life, we prefer to make up our minds about people through personal acquaintance and observation rather than on the basis of others' reports.)

If we think of the most memorable literary characters we probably find that we remember them doing or saying things, we do not so much remember being told things about them. And where a narrative comment on a character does stick in our minds then it is probably as a result of something other than characterization; irony, moral discrimination, or whatever.

So far as the creation of lifelike characters is concerned, it is very often the interplay between given and explained attributes that makes them fascinating: think of Heathcliff in *Wuthering Heights*; we understand partly why he is as he is because we have witnessed key elements of his upbringing. But there are some elements that seem to be beyond such an explanation.

Creating a lifelike character may not, however, be what a novelist is always aiming at. It is not lifelike for Gulliver to be so acute and humane at one part of *Gulliver's Travels* and so obtuse and irresponsive to talk of human suffering at others. But it seems apparent that Swift's primary aim here is not the creation of a consistent and lifelike character so much as the creation of a character whose alternating qualities and abilities will represent different aspects of that 'human race' that is perhaps the real subject of *Gulliver's Travels*.

What are the most important methods of characterization available to the novelist? I would suggest four that are worth thinking about. First by *description* or *report*. In Conrad's *Heart of Darkness* we know a very large amount about Mr Kurtz before he ever appears before us; other characters in the novella have talked about him so much, have reported on his actions and beliefs, that we feel it is almost as if we had met him ourselves.

Secondly by *action*; when Insarov in Turgenev's *On the Eve* (1859) throws the insolent German into the water – an action of which his effete Russian companions are palpably incapable –

then we learn something about him which pages of description could not give us.

Thirdly through a character's *thought* or *conversation*. Dialogue in particular is a wonderful way of revealing character: think how much we learn about Miss Bates in *Emma* merely through her conversation – so much so that comment from Austen's narrator is really not needed. Modern novelists have shown how much we can learn about a character merely by following his or her thoughts; in Virginia Woolf's *Mrs Dalloway* Clarissa Dalloway and Peter Walsh actually *do* very little, but by the end of the novel we feel that we know them quite well just by having following so many of their thoughts.

In the third paragraph of chapter 2 of Jane Austen's *Sense and Sensibility* (1811) we learn as much as we feel we need to learn about Mrs John Dashwood through a report of her comments on her husband's intended generosity to his two sisters. Austen here uses Free Indirect Speech (discussed earlier in my section on narrative technique), and as this is frequently used for ironic purposes we are alert to the hints concerning the narrator's disapproval without their ever becoming overt and intruding directly.

Mrs John Dashwood did not at all approve of what her husband intended to do for his sisters. To take three thousand pounds from the fortune of their dear little boy, would be impoverishing him to the most dreadful degree. She begged him to think again on the subject. How could he answer it to himself to rob his child, and his only child too, of so large a sum? And what possible claim could the Miss Dashwoods, who were related to him only by half blood, which she considered as no relationship at all, have on his generosity to so large an amount. It was very well known that no affection was ever supposed to exist between the children of any man by different marriages; and why was he to ruin himself, and their poor little Harry, by giving away all his money to his half sisters?

The pleasure we get from such a passage is related to the fact that while on the one hand we do not feel we are being told how to regard Mrs John Dashwood and coerced into a particular attitude towards her, we also feel that our amused disapproval of the character is shared by Jane Austen (through her narrative voice). The very omission of comment on the more outrageous statements of Mrs John Dashwood's indicates a narrative opinion that they *are* so outrageous as to require no comment.

And finally the novelist can use *symbol* or *image* to reveal and develop a character. In Jean Rhys's novel *After Leaving Mr Mackenzie* (1930) the heroine, Julia, has just been to see a Mr James, shortly after visiting her dying mother and her spinsterish sister Norah:

She wanted to cry as he went down the stairs with her. She thought: 'That wasn't what I wanted.' She had hoped that he would say something or look something that would make her feel less lonely.

There was a vase of flame-coloured tulips in the hall – surely the most graceful of flowers. Some thrust their heads forward like snakes, and some were very erect, stiff, virginal, rather prim. Some were dying, with curved grace in their death.

The tulips present us symbolically with the different options we have seen women in the novel plump for: snake-like cunning and self-interested behaviour; prim and virginal lifelessness (like Norah); and death – like Julia's mother. Such a passage contributes to our knowledge of and attitudes to characters in the novel even though nothing is said directly about any character.

One final point. We should not assume that because we can respond so fully to characters in the fiction of past ages there is, therefore, no change in fictional characterization from age to age. Not only are there technical changes in the way novelists learn to create and reveal characters, but changes in human beings outside literature (or at least the belief that human beings have changed) often lead novelists to use new methods to produce a new sort of character. Thus in her famous essay 'Mr Bennett and Mrs Brown' (1924) Virginia Woolf makes the part tongue-in-cheek remark that 'in or about December, 1910, human character changed.' Woolf is of course exaggerating for humorous and other purposes, but it is clear that she is serious in the main point that she makes in the essay, that changes in human beings have taken place, and thus changes in the ways novelists represent human beings must also occur. Thus if we feel tempted to complain (as many *have* complained) that characters in the *nouveau roman* are less satisfying than those in Dickens's novels, we should pause to ask whether or not we would be happy with a situation in which the contemporary novel used only the characterization of Dickens. Would the novel help us to understand contemporary human beings if that were the case?

(iii) Plot

Let us start with a definition: a plot is an ordered, organized sequence of events and actions. Plots in this sense are found in novels rather than in ordinary life; life has stories, but novels have plots and stories. As E.M. Forster puts it, a story is a narrative of events arranged in their time-sequence, whereas a plot is a narrative of events with the emphasis falling on *causality*. Not all commentators would agree that causality is the distinguishing feature, but all would agree that there is a necessary distinction to be made between the incidents about which we are told in a novel in their chronological order, and the actual narrating of these events in perhaps quite a different order in the novel. I prefer the terms 'story' and 'plot' to describe these two, but some critics use terms created by a group of theorists known as the Russian Formalists, the terms 'sjužet' (story) and 'fabula' (plot).

If you have read William Faulkner's novel *Absalom, Absalom!* and Jean Rhys's novel *Wide Sargasso Sea* it may have struck you that the stories in both novels are remarkably similar (which you can confirm if you wish by writing them both down in chronological order). But the two plots are very different, so different that the similarity of the stories is not immediately apparent.[13]

Again, if you have read Joseph Conrad's novel *Nostromo* (1904) you will know that it has a very complex plot; the novel *could* have been told in a far more straightforward, chronological way. So why did Conrad tell it in such a complicated, *un*chronological manner? Come to that, why did Emily Brontë not have *Wuthering Heights* told to us in one consistent chronological sweep – perhaps by having Nelly Dean recount it all at one meeting to Mr Lockwood?

The answer to such questions has to be complex. A novelist constructs a plot in a particular manner so as to draw attention to certain things which might otherwise escape notice, to produce a different effect upon the reader, and so on. One result of the complex plot of *Nostromo*, for example, is that Conrad deliberately kills what many novelists strive for: tension and reader expectation. We know from early on in the novel what the eventual outcome of the political and military struggles in Costaguana will be. Why does he do this? One likely reason is that as the reader has to devote less attention or expectation to *what* will happen, he or she is able to devote much more to *why* and *how* it happens. Tension may make us read quickly and carelessly, anxious only to find out what happens. Such a reading is discouraged by the way *Nostromo* is constructed. It is encouraged, in contrast, by the way in which most of Dickens's novels are constructed; Dickens wants to engage our sympathetic anxiety and so he sets puzzles, creates mysteries which we read on in order to solve.

If a novelist abandons strict chronology, how else can he or she retain coherence, make the novel hang together? Well, as Forster points out, *causality* is one important possible way. We are still interested as we read the final chapters of *Nostromo* because we see why things happen as they do; causal links are revealed to us.

Apart from causality, a novelist can draw *parallels* and *resemblances* between characters, situations and events such that the novel has coherence even if it plots neither chronological sequences nor causal relationships. It is only to a limited degree that we believe that the experiences of the second-generation characters in *Wuthering Heights* are caused by the lives and actions of the first-generation characters. But the parallels (with variations) and resemblances between the younger Cathy, Linton Heathcliff, and Hareton Earnshaw and their parents make us feel that this latter part of the novel continues themes and enquiries from the first part of the novel.

Alternatively, a novel can be held together by a common character or event. The picaresque novel is held together by the character of the picaro, for instance. This is a relatively crude form of unity, and has seemed generally inadequate to many later novelists.

It should be said that with modernism and post-modernism the whole question as to whether a novel *should* compose a unity has been subjected to considerable sceptical doubt. Virginia Woolf argued against plot (in the sense of the traditional, well-structured, realist plot) as one of a number of distorting conventions in her essay 'Modern Fiction' (1919), and a novel such as Alain Robbe-Grillet's *The Voyeur* (1955) certainly lacks unifying elements as we have outlined them. The actual denial of causality as a reliable principle by many modernist and post-modernist novelists has, inevitably, affected the way they construct their novels.

Let me say a few words concerning *types of plot*. This is not intended as a dull exercise in categorizing, but as a means of indicating the different principles that can lie behind a novel's plot. We can describe plots in two ways: either in terms of the dominant human activities which form the motivating principle in them or which are induced in the reader by them, or in more technical ways. In the first category we can include plots structured around *conflict* as in many ways the plot of *Nostromo* is; around *mystery* as many of Dickens's novels are; around *pursuit* or *search* as is *The Castle*; around a *journey* as is *Gulliver's Travels*; or, finally, around a *test* like Joseph Conrad's *The Shadow-Line*. Now of course these are very simplistic descriptions and we would want to say that all of these novels were structured around far more complex issues than the single topics mentioned. But it is worthwhile remembering that a novel is often given force and coherence by a dominating element such as one of these plot types provides. *The Shadow-Line* is much more than just a test, but the theme of the test is a sort of archetypal bedrock within the organizing logic of the plot, and we should not be ashamed to see it as such.

A more technical classification of plots will provide us with terms like 'picaresque/episodic'; 'well-made' (the traditional nineteenth-century realist plot)'; 'multiple' (many novels have two or more lines of plot, sometimes interconnecting and sometimes not. It is very often important to be able to single out a *main plot* from its attendant *sub plot(s)* for the purpose of analysis.)

You may recall that much earlier on in this book I quoted Johnson's remark that if one were to read Richardson 'for the story' then one would be so fretted that one would hang one-self. Plot and story fulfil different sorts of functions in different novels; according to Johnson the story in a novel by Richardson is there only to give occasion to the sentiment; in other novels the tension and suspense relative to our desire to know 'what happens next' are an integral part of the appeal of the work. When the 'outer' narrator of *Heart of Darkness* warns us (indirectly) that we are about to hear 'about one of Marlow's inconclusive experiences' then we need to adjust our expectations with regard to the plot of the novella. We should not expect a 'well-made plot' with growing tension culminating in a climax and a final resolution that solves everything – as in a typical Dickens novel. Modernist fiction typically does have inconclusive endings, endings which leave the reader perhaps puzzled and unsatisfied, but puzzled and unsatisfied in ways that are productive of further thought. We should not reject such plots merely because they do not give us that satisfaction that the plot of a novel like *Our Mutual Friend* (1864–5) gives us; Dickens's plots have their own dissatisfactions (the perhaps too-easy machinery for the resolution of problems, the inevitable punishment of the wicked and reward of the good) of which we may become increasingly aware the more we read works such as *Heart of Darkness* or *The Castle*.

(iv) Structure

Structure and *plot* are closely related to each other, and it might have made sense to include this section as a sub-section of 'Plot'. But the term 'structure' does, properly, refer to something rather different from plot. If we can think of the plot of a novel as the way in which its story is arranged, its structure involves more than its story, encompassing the work's total organization as a piece of literature, a work of art. Nor are the terms 'structure' and 'form' to be confused; the latter term does not normally include thematic elements in the work (see my comments later on concerning 'theme') whereas these are involved in a novel's structure. Structure involves plot, thematics, and form: it refers to our sense of a novel's overall organization and patterning, the way in which its component parts fit together to produce a totality, a satisfying whole – or, of course, the way in which they fail so to do.

Let us start by observing that different novels have very different sorts of structure. We feel, for example, that some parts of *Moll Flanders* or *Huckleberry Finn* could be shifted around in position without making too great a difference to the works in question: how many readers of the former work remember clearly whether Moll robbed the little girl of her necklace before or after she robbed the drunken man in the coach? But to shuffle around the parts of *Wuthering Heights*, or of Henry James's *What Maisie knew* (1897) would, we feel, do something rather serious to the works in question.

Clearly the fact that a novel has an *episodic* structure has an important bearing upon such issues; if a work is structured around a series of relatively self-contained episodes, then these can be assembled in different orders without making too much difference – just as on a modular degree scheme with self-contained modules one can often take different courses in any order one chooses.

But the matter goes beyond plot, as I have suggested. In *Moll Flanders* there is very little alteration in Moll's character, or in the values the narrative underwrites, or in the symbolic meanings contained in the work (if there are any worth noting in this novel!). In short, *Moll Flanders* is consistently structured on the principle of 'repetition-with-slight-variation'. There is somewhat more development and change in *Huckleberry Finn* – in the characters and relationship of Huck and Jim, in the general *tone* of the novel subsequent upon the experiences Huck has, and so on. Thus although some of the scenes in this novel might be switched around without too much effect, such alteration would have to be more limited than with *Moll Flanders* if we wished to avoid damaging the work. But the intricate patterning of a novel such as *What Maisie Knew* would, surely, be completely destroyed if we started to move sections of it from place to place.

Very often the *chapter* and *section* divisions made by the author impose a structure upon a work – or bring out one that is implicit but not overt in it already. It is interesting to read Conrad's *The Shadow-Line* in his manuscript version, in which there are no section divisions, and then to see how differently the published text of the novel reads with these divisons included. Very often such divisions perform the useful function of telling the reader when he or she can pause and put the book down for a bit, and as it is at these points of time that we think backwards over what we have read and forwards to what we hope for or expect, such divisions can be very significant. It is doubtless for such reasons that Virginia Woolf disapproved of the 'ill-fitting vestments' of the 'two and thirty chapters' of what she called the materialist novel (in her essay 'Modern Fiction').

Order and *chronology* – issues upon which we touched when talking of plot – are crucial to the matter of structure. The difference between a novel's 'story' and its 'plot' can tell us much about its structure. It is often an interesting exercise to map out a novel's story and plot in note form one above the other. Think how important it is, for example, that we start *Wuthering Heights* at exactly the point we do: we go into the results of the experiences that dominate the novel in these opening pages, and then trace their roots and their resolution. It is crucial to this novel that we meet the adult, embittered but successful Heathcliff before we meet him as a child or as a young lover.

But structure as I said involves thematic elements too. Note how the repetition of thematic elements in Charles Dickens's *Bleak House* helps to structure that work. Just to take one example: Esther Summerson, like her mother Lady Dedlock, has to choose between two men: a rich, older, 'safe' one and a younger, less wealthy, more 'risky' match. But whereas Lady Dedlock makes what we are led to see as the wrong choice in marrying the older man, Esther – after an initial false decision – makes what is clearly the right decision for her. Now this produces an element of *pattern* in the work which contributes to our sense of its structure, a pattern which blends in with other things in *Bleak House* to produce a satisfying work of art.

Take a different example. In Katherine Mansfield's short story 'The Voyage' we have a very simple plot: a little girl leaves her father at a New Zealand port and travels by boat with her grandmother to the other island of New Zealand, to her grandparents' home. In the course of the voyage we discover that her mother has died, and the reader assumes what Fenella – the girl – has not yet realized: that she is to be brought up henceforth by her grandparents. What is striking about the story is that whereas images of darkness and cold dominate the opening of the story, these gradually give way to images of light and warmth which (especially the images of light) dominate the close of the story. Now clearly this shift of images contributes to the structure of the story: without actually being told it directly we realize that Fenella is moving out of an unhappy period of her life into a potentially much happier one: structurally the voyage is not just from one *place* to another, but this is complemented by travel from one *state* to another.

Structure involves ideas and sensations of some sort of pattern: *completion, reiteration, contrast, repetition, complementarity* – all of these and others can be invoked in us by a work's structure. And we should note that the *frame* of a narrative – what constitutes its outer limits – can contribute importantly to our sense of structure. Consider the narrative framing of the 'tale within a tale' of *Heart of Darkness* and *The Turn of the Screw*. Think of the importance of the fact that James Joyce's *Ulysses* and Virginia Woolf's *Mrs Dalloway* take place within twenty-four hours. Note the thematic framing effect of our being told in E.M. Forster's novel *Howards End* that the work is not to be concerned with the very poor, who are 'unthinkable'. In each case our view of what is 'in' the novel is given structure by our sense of what is excluded from it.

(v) Setting

'Setting' is one of those terms about which recent literary critics have felt increasingly uneasy. Does the term not suggest a perhaps too-simple relationship between characters and action on the one hand and the context within which these take place on the other? Doesn't it sound rather unsatisfactory to talk about the Nottinghamshire 'setting' of D.H. Lawrence's *Sons and Lovers* or the Yorkshire 'setting' of *Wuthering Heights*, as if the same actions might conceivably have taken place elsewhere – in Tunbridge Wells or Minnesota? The fact that so many characters in Emily Brontë's novel have names that are also the place-names of towns and villages around her native Haworth suggests a relationship between character and environment too organic, we feel, to be described with the term 'setting'.

And yet it is important to be aware of the context within which the action of a novel takes place – and this does not just mean its geographical setting; social and historical factors are also important.

To start with we need to distinguish between realistic and conventional or stylized settings. The famous country-house of the classic detective story is obviously a highly *conventional* setting; we are not interested in the particularity of such country houses and their environments, they serve, rather, the function of providing a stylized and familiar setting within which a conventional set of happenings can unfold.

At the other extreme we can cite highly realistic settings like that of the tuberculosis sanatorium that dominates Thomas Mann's *The Magic Mountain*. Here, however, we need to tread carefully, for although this may be a realistic setting it is also a very *symbolic* one as well. It is not hard to see the sanatorium full of sick people as representative of pre-First-World-War Europe with its sicknesses and fatal illnesses. Authors are very often quite conscious of such symbolic meanings; in his essay 'Well Done' (1918) Joseph Conrad refers to 'the ship' as 'the moral symbol of our life', and clearly we need to take such a statement into account when looking at those of his works which are set on board ship.

Sometimes the choice of a suitable setting helps an author to avoid the need to write about things that he or she is not good at, or interested in, writing about. It was convenient for Conrad, for instance, that his ships often contained no women. A setting in the historical past can often help an author to avoid contemporary issues about which he or she feels confused; the setting that E.M. Forster chooses for *Howards End* enabled him to avoid writing about the very poor. It is generally agreed that Jane Austen chose settings for her novels which were perfect in terms of their allowing her to exercise her strengths and conceal her weaknesses so far as her knowledge of different sorts of people and of human experiences was concerned.

Moreover, Dickens's frequent choice of London as setting for his novels was convenient in other ways: the mass of concealed relationships, indirect forms of human communication, and innumerable secrets were perfect for a novelist whose plots contain all of these elements in like abundance.

It is important to note that a setting can be a crucial factor in the creation of *mood* or *moral environment*. (Note that *mood* here is being used in its ordinary sense, and not in the technical sense outlined above in the discussion of narrative technique. To avoid possible confusion I prefer to reserve the term *mode* for discussions involving narrative technique.)

If we think of *The Great Gatsby* we can see, I think, how a setting can make an essential contribution to a work's mood. And this example reminds us that theme and subject and setting can be inextricably intertwined: you could no more set *The Great Gatsby* in 1930s Salford than you could set Walter Greenwood's *Love on the Dole* (1933) anywhere else.

Remember that there is a difference, in this context, between 'mood' and 'tone', as the latter term involves narrative *attitudes towards* what is recounted and described. A given setting may help to create a particular mood in a story, but only the narrative treatment can confirm a certain tone.

(vi) Theme

'Theme' is a much used word in the literary criticism of the novel, and a favourite word for use by lecturers and teachers in essay and examination questions. 'Discuss the treatment of the theme of evil in *Crime and Punishment*'; 'Write about the theme of escape in *Huckleberry Finn*'; '. . . the theme of alienation in Franz Kafka's *The Castle*', and so on.

Students often find such questions or topics baffling. What exactly *is* a theme? Well, the confusing answer to this question is that the term is used in a number of different ways.

Firstly we should note that a theme may be overt or covert, that is to say it can be either consciously intended and indicated as such by the author, or alternatively, discovered by the reader/critic as an element in the novel of which perhaps even the author was unaware. Thus although we can be pretty certain that Saul Bellow had the *carpe diem* theme ('Live today, while you can') consciously in mind in his novella *Seize the Day* (1956) – because the title makes this much clear – we cannot be so sure that Alan Sillitoe had the theme of working-class socialization equally in mind with regard to the writing of his *Saturday Night and Sunday Morning* (1958). (And we should also bear in mind the possibility that Bellow recognized his theme and chose his title after he had completed writing his story.)

So far as Sillitoe's novel is concerned, a sociologist could certainly look at it and detect the process whereby a rebellious working-class young man is led in representative stages to accept norms of behaviour, attitudes and institutions which most young working-class men in Britain in the late 1940s and 1950s *were* led to accept. But as to whether Sillitoe consciously intends this, and whether it is an overt theme of the novel is a matter for debate. (Given the novel's origin in a number of discrete pieces it seems rather unlikely.)

We can also distinguish between concepts of theme which see it as a 'central idea' and those which view it more as a 'recurrent argument, claim, doctrine, or issue'. This distinction hinges upon the extent to which a novel is seen not just to *contain* a particular element, but also to put forward a case for a point of view or established position. If we define theme in the former, weaker sense then we will not be surprised to discover that a large and complex novel can have a range of varied themes attributed to it. Charles Dickens's *Bleak House*, for instance, has been variously interpreted as containing the themes of 'parental responsibility', 'the heartlessness of the law', 'the evil of "causes"', 'the destructiveness of choosing money and position rather than love', 'the centrality of writing to Victorian society' – and many more. It needs to be remembered that a complex novel will certainly be susceptible of analysis in terms of a large number of different – perhaps interlocking – themes. All of the aforementioned themes *can* be found in *Bleak House*, but the reader must decide what their relative force and importance in the novel are.

(vii) Symbol and image

Let us introduce this section with some concrete examples. In E.M. Forster's *Howards End* the motor-car plays an important rôle. We could respond to this fact by pointing out that the car had not been around for very long at the time that the novel was written, and that Forster was merely incorporating a piece of contemporary reality into his novel for the purpose of increased verisimilitude.

Few readers of the work would find this satisfactory as an explanation. The motor-car in *Howards End* clearly *stands for* or *represents* something; it is not merely a means of transport but a *symbol* in the novel. By this we mean that it carries with it various ideas, associations, forms of significance that in ordinary life it might not have in people's minds: 'the new and destructive of the traditional'; 'the mechanical as against the organic'; 'unfeeling social change'; 'violence and death'; 'the selfish pursuit of personal comfort by the rich' – and so on.

Notice that I have not suggested that the car in *Howards End* stands for just one, fixed thing; it is characteristic of symbols that they do not have a simple one-to-one relationship with what they stand for or suggest. The lighthouse in Virginia Woolf's *To the Lighthouse* (1927) has a fairly obvious symbolic force in the novel, but it would be an unwise critic who stated definitively the one thing that it stood for. Perhaps the lighthouse does stand for the unfulfilled dreams of youth, or masculine aggressiveness – but part of its power comes from its multiple suggestiveness and indirect significance.

Symbols are not limited to literature and art: they are central to all known human cultures. When a woman gets married in white she makes use of the symbolic force of that colour for dress within our culture – a symbolic force that has existed for an extremely long time. Any writer who made use of this fact in a novel would be taking what we can call a public symbol and adapting it for use within his or her work.

Thus in James Joyce's story 'The Dead' (started 1907, published 1915) we feel that the repeated references to snow have a symbolic force. This is partly because snow is referred to so repetitively and suggestively that the reader of the story cannot but feel that there is something significant in the function that snow performs in the story. But it is also, of course, because we naturally associate snow with some things rather than others – especially in countries like Britain and Ireland where extensive falls of snow are relatively rare. Put briefly we can suggest that in 'The Dead' snow stands for or suggests *death*: it is cold, it covers the graveyard, it affects the whole country as death comes to us all, and so on. Now the justification for this interpretation is partly that snow is naturally associated with death, because it is cold like a dead body, and because people lost in snow die. But it is partly because Joyce in 'The Dead' draws attention to certain of these qualities and associates them with other references in the story (not least with its title) so as to make these associations clear. If we think of the death of Gerald in the snow in D.H. Lawrence's *Women in Love* we will see, I think, that both Joyce and Lawrence are able to incorporate a public symbol into the private or internal world of meaning of their respective fictional works.

But on occasions a writer will create a symbol that has the meaning and significance that it does have only in the context of one particular work. If we think of a green light, for instance, the natural symbolic associations that it has for most of us today are positive: advance, road clear, optimism – all of those extensions of meaning that have accrued from our use of green lights in traffic regulation systems. But it is arguable that none of these references or associations are active in our response to the repeated mention of the green light that marks out the quay by Daisy's house for Gatsby in Scott Fitzgerald's *The Great Gatsby*. What Fitzgerald succeeds in doing in this novel is to create a private symbol, something that has meaning only within the world of the novel. Similarly, it is arguable that few if any of the public symbolic associations of lighthouses are active within Virginia Woolf's *To the Lighthouse*; the significance of the lighthouse in that work (and by this I mean the significance for the reader – which is not necessarily the significance we are to presume it has for characters in the novel) is something that has to be decided upon the basis of internal rather than public information.

Another set of terms for public and private symbols is *motivated* and *unmotivated* symbols. In practice, of course, it's hard to find a completely public or a completely private symbol. I suggested, for example, that E.M. Forster's use of the motor-car in *Howards End* developed associations that 'motor-car' might not have in people's minds prior to their reading the novel. But it is clear that *some* people *might* have made these associations, and that the symbolic force that the motor-car has in *Howards End* is, as it were, a potential force already implicit in the motor-car as it was experienced in Edwardian England. (Think of the significance of the motor-car in a work of fiction that is near-contemporary to Forster's: Kenneth Grahame's *The Wind in the Willows* [1908].)

And when Henry James uses a beautiful and expensive but flawed bowl as a symbol in *The Golden Bowl* (1904) we can understand, I think, that this offers itself as a more obvious symbol of a marriage containing a guilty secret than a packet of peanuts or a scotch egg. The flawed bowl is thus a more motivated symbol than is the green light in *The Great Gatsby*.

Let us pass from symbols to images. I referred earlier to Katherine Mansfield's short story 'The Voyage', and commented upon the movement from dark and cold references at the start of the story to warm and – particularly – light images at the end of the story. Let me quote a little from the end of the story.

On the table a white cat, that had been folded up like a camel, rose, stretched itself, yawned, and then sprang on to the tips of its toes. Fenella buried one cold little hand in the white, warm fur, and smiled timidly while she stroked and listened to Grandma's gentle voice and the rolling tones of Grandpa.

A door creaked. 'Come in, dear.' There, lying to one side of an immense bed, lay Grandpa. Just his head with a white tuft, and his rosy face and long silver beard showed over the quilt.

You will notice the recurrence of words that connote lightness and warmth here ('white', 'warm', 'silver', 'rosy'). These I would dub *images* rather than symbols. The distinction is not an easy one to explain, and there are differences of usage that complicate matters, but the following points are probably worth remembering.

1 Images are usually characterized by *concrete qualities* rather than abstract meanings; images normally have a more sensuous quality than symbols – they call the taste, smell, feel, sound or visual image of the referred-to object sharply to mind.

2 Symbols, in contrast, because they *stand for* something other than themselves bring to mind not their own concrete qualities so much as the idea or abstraction that is associated with them.

Thus in the extract from Katherine Mansfield the feel of the cat's fur, its whiteness and warmth, are brought sharply to our minds *in themselves* – we do not automatically wonder what they 'stand for' (note how this tactile sense is encouraged by the contrast with Fenella's cold hand.) But we do not experience sharp sensory responses to Gatsby's green light or Woolf's lighthouse: it is what these stand for or call to mind *apart from themselves* that is important. With Joyce's snow and Forster's motor-car we may pause: I think that in these cases we think both of what they stand for but also of their individual sensory qualities. In these two cases, therefore, we may guess that the references have an imagistic function alongside their primary symbolic purpose.

This is not to say, incidentally, that images do not contribute to thematic elements in a work. Although it is true that an image is distinguished by its concrete qualities in an immediate sense, it sets up waves of association in the mind that have other than a purely concrete significance. Thus, as I have already suggested, the images in Mansfield's 'The Voyage' contribute importantly to our sense of the multi-levelled nature of Fenella's voyage, away from unhappiness and suffering and to the promise of something a lot more cheerful and enjoyable.

(viii) Speech and dialogue

Modern readers are fortunate in that they live in an age of tape-recorders. They can thus study normal, unselfconscious conversation in a way that our ancestors could not – and they can thereby discover that nobody actually talks quite as people are represented as talking in novels. Any transcription of an interview will give us something that looks very different from what we are used to reading in a novel – and yet when we read novels the dialogue in them seems realistic. Why is this?

The answer has to be that the novelist follows conventions in the representation of speech and dialogue with which we are so familiar that we are unaware of any conventionality. (Just as we are unaware that we follow conventions governing the nodding and the shaking of heads to mean 'yes' and 'no' – until we travel to a country like Turkey or Bulgaria where these conventions are reversed.) People in novels tend to talk in complete sentences, with few indicated hesitations, mistakes of grammar, 'ums' and 'ers', and so on.

The novelist has to convey exclusively in words what in ordinary conversation we convey by words, tone of voice, hesitations, facial expression, gesture, bodily posture – and by other means. Learning how to do so was not accomplished overnight, and we can note a great difference between the way novelists in the eighteenth century represented dialogue and the way later novelists have done so. If, for example, you open Henry Fielding's novel *Joseph Andrews* (1742) at Chapter 5, which is the chapter directly parodying Richardson's *Pamela* in which Lady Booby attempts to seduce her servant Joseph as Mr B– in Richardsons's novel had attempted to seduce Pamela, then you will notice something odd about the layout of the page. Although conversation takes place all through this short chapter, the prose is set out in one continuous unparagraphed stream. Thus Fielding has to keep including 'tag-phrases' such as 'he said' and 'she replied'. The result is not just that reading the chapter is rather hard work, but that the guiding presence of the narrator keeps intruding: we have narrative tag-phrases in adition to the actual words spoken by the characters.

If we move to Jane Austen's *Pride and Prejudice* (1813, but written 1796/7) we see a very different picture. Dialogue is presented in a recognizably modern form, with each new utterance by a different character given a new paragraph. Here the narrator may intrude or remain hidden at will. If necessary the characters can be left to speak for themselves with no interruption from anyone. This certainly increases the *dramatic* effectiveness of scenes involving dialogue; we feel more that we are actually witnessing conversations take place rather than being instructed by an intrusive stage-manager who keeps pointing out what we have to notice.

The narrator can now use the different possibilities available to create an appropriate effect. Take the conversation between Mr Bennet and his wife that we are given on the first page of *Pride and Prejudice*.

'My dear Mr Bennet,' said his lady to him one day, 'have you heard that Netherfield Park is let at last?'

Mr Bennet replied that he had not.

'But it is,' returned she; 'for Mrs Long has just been here, and she told me all about it.'

Mr Bennet made no answer.

'Do not you want to know who has taken it?' cried his wife impatiently.

'*You* want to tell me, and I have no objection to hearing it.'

This was invitation enough.

Note how Jane Austen wrings so much significance out of her use of Direct and Indirect Speech here. 'Mr Bennet replied that he had not' must be one of the most economically sarcastic lines in English literature: the shift to Indirect Speech somehow conjures up Mr Bennet's weary, long-suffering response to his wife's importuning. We can see that the narrative comments here are more like touches on the tiller than fuller-scale intrusions; we feel that we are witnessing a real conversation but with someone beside us whispering in our ear comments concerning the participants in the discussion.

7   Studying the Novel

Studying the novel is different from reading a novel, although I hope that the result of studying novels for you will be that you will be able to read novels with more pleasure than before. To study the novel means, in part, being conscious in your reading of some of the things that I have been talking about in this book up to now, but it does not just mean this.

When we read a novel we may do it with a shortish novel in one sitting, or in anything up to twenty or more sittings with a long and complex novel like Tolstoy's *War and Peace*. For those readers who read Victorian novels when they were first published in serial form there was no choice: they *had* to stop and wait at certain stages in their reading. When we pause in our reading of a novel we go over what we have read and we think forward to what we guess will happen or what we would like to happen. Frequently we will imagine ourselves in situations described in the novel; perhaps we will hold imaginary conversations with characters, or wonder what we might have done in their positions.

Put another way: expectation, surprise, disappointment, foreboding, tension, suspense, imagination, fantasy – all these form part of our reading of a novel. To read a novel is to partake in a *cumulative process*.

The problem which this raises for the study of the novel is that there are certain experiences in us, and certain events in the novel, which lodge far more permanently in the mind than do others. Indeed, it is part of the way that a novel works upon us – part of its power as a source of enjoyment – that some aspects of our reading experience should fade more quickly than others. Moreover, our memory plays tricks with us once we have finished a novel. If it is some time since you read

Wuthering Heights then try this test on yourself: at what stage in the novel does the older Catherine die? I suspect that unless you are an unusually retentive and conscientious reader you are likely to place this event far later in the novel than it actually occurs.

The issue is complicated by the fact that we often read a novel more than once. One of the distinguishing features of good novels (unlike pulp fiction) is that we can get something new out of a second or third reading of the same piece of fiction. On a subsequent reading we are normally less preoccupied with what will happen and so are able to read more carefully and notice all sorts of detail that slipped our attention on first reading.

So to *study* a novel we need to find ways of preserving things that would otherwise be lost. To do this we first of all have to notice these things. I hope that the earlier part of this book will have suggested to you all sorts of things that you can be looking out for and noticing while you are reading a novel, things in yourself, in your own responses, as much as in the novel itself.

In ordinary life when we want to preserve something we use aids: holiday photographs, diaries, memo-pads, and so on. And to study the novel we have to do the same. We need to take notes. Taking notes is actually a skilled operation and one which one has to practise in order to be good at it. And it takes time before one can develop one's skill to the point at which it does not interfere with one's reading. So here are some suggestions.

(i) How to take notes

One can write notes either in the novel one is reading or in a separate notebook. The advantage of the former method is that it does not disturb one's reading too much; the disadvantage is that it spoils a book, it affects one's second reading of the novel, there is not always too much room for notes in the book, and *retrieval* of the notes afterwards for purposes of study is difficult. One way round these problems is to write very brief notes in pencil in a novel as one is reading, and then to copy these up and expand them in a separate notebook or folder later on. This also allows one to copy out brief extracts from the novel which strike one as important, and it means that you file for future reference only notes about which you have thought a second time after having finished reading the novel. One's pencil marks can be erased once they have served their purpose.

If something in the text strikes you as important or significant but you don't want to puzzle over why lest you break your train of thought then mark or underline the passage in question, note the page reference on the inside back cover of the book, and come back to ponder the point once you have finished the novel.

(ii) What to note

Learning what is of significance in a novel, and in your response to it, is a matter of practice. Teachers and lecturers often ask for analyses of selected passages from novels, and undertaking such analyses is an excellent way of sharpening your eye for important detail in the reading of fiction. Such close reading is, however, only part of what constitutes a full critical reading of a novel, for in addition to responding to significant detail in the prose of a work of fiction you need also to be able to perceive larger patterns and movements in the work as a whole, as well as connections to other works. The list that follows is intended to serve a double purpose. On the one hand I hope that it will be useful to work from when you are engaged in the analysis of a particular passage from a novel or a short story. In addition, however, I hope that its perusal will serve as a reminder of the sort of points that can be noted in the process of reading or rereading a work of fiction. The golden rule here is: if in doubt, then make a note. An unnecessary or misguided note can be discarded, but a note not taken may turn out to be irretrievable.

Checklist

- *Narrative technique*: all information relating to the manipulation of point of view in the work: clues about the values or personality of the narrator or narrative perspective; any indication that there are some things the narrator *doesn't* know; changes of narrator or narrative perspective; narrative intrusion or comment. 'Telling' and 'Showing'.
- *Tone*: is it familiar or formal, intimate or impersonal? Who

(if anyone) is apparently being addressed? Do the vocabulary or syntax suggest a particular style of delivery?

- *Characterization*: information about *how* we learn about characters; any indication that characters are changing or developing; significant new information about a character.
- *Speech and dialogue*: use of Direct, Indirect or Free Indirect Speech. Do characters speak for themselves or does the narrator intrude and comment? Is the dialogue realistic or conventional? What functions does it perform? (Development of character, of plot, introduction of dramatic element, discussion of theme(s).)
- *Thoughts/mental processes*: Do we 'get inside characters' heads'? If so, how?
- *Dramatic involvement*: is the reader drawn into events as they happen, or rather encouraged to observe them dispassionately? How is this achieved?
- *Action*: any information that advances the plot, gives significant new developments in human relationships or new events.
- *Symbol or image*: anything apparently significant should be noted. Do symbols/images relate to others used elsewhere in the work?
- *Theme(s)*: any development of themes dealt with elsewhere in the work; introduction of new thematic elements. Moral problems/issues raised for the characters or for the reader.
- *Your own response*: strong personal preferences/ responses the work evokes in you – or dislikes/ disapproval. Strong identification with a character – or the opposite. Tension, desire to know what happens. Particular expectations (especially at the end of chapters/ sections, or when a mystery or problem is presented). Any experience of bafflement or surprise; and points where you feel you disagree with or react against a narrative opinion (or the opinion of a character).

(iii) Revision

If you have taken full notes from your reading of novels and your study of critics then the process of revision should be easier for you. Always study your notes in conjunction with the novel concerned; it makes no sense to memorize a set of notes if you have forgotten the salient details from the work itself.

You may take an examination requiring knowledge of a number of novels up to a year after you have read some of them. Full rereading is impossible, and some elements will certainly have slipped your memory. *Don't* try to skip-read the whole work again (unless it is a short story), but concentrate upon reading selected passages with care. These should always include the opening and closing pages of the work – beginnings and endings of novels are invariably revealing. Is the opening dramatic or descriptive? Does it plunge the reader into the middle of things, or carefully establish a scene? Does it set a dominant tone, and establish the narrative perspective or personality of the narrator? Is the reader addressed directly, and are we given an indication of how the narrator conceives of the reader? Is the ending happy or sad (and why does the author choose to make it so?) Does it tie up all the loose ends or leave many questions unanswered? (And with what effect?)

Apart from opening and closing pages, you should pick some key passages – either those that have seemed important to you, or those which critics have found of great interest. And pick a couple of passages at random, preferably ones that seem unfamiliar on leafing through the work. Analyse these in detail.

If it makes you feel easier then construct a list of character names (just the main characters) for each work prior to an examination. But if you forget a name in an examination don't panic, just leave a blank and go on writing. If the name doesn't come to you by the end of the examination then asterisk the gap and write in a footnote explaining that you have forgotten the character name and indicating who the character is by other means such as relationships to other characters.

8 Critical Approaches to Fiction

The following survey is designed to help students in a number of different ways. Firstly, I hope that it will make *recognition* of different critical approaches easier. (By a critical approach I mean both the underlying theoretical assumptions of the critic concerned, but also his or her particular methods of analysis and inquiry.) Such recognition may not be easy, as although it is relatively easy to describe a critical approach in rather abstract and general terms, particular critics often combine a number of different assumptions and methods in their critical work.

Secondly, I hope that the following brief survey will help you to think about the variety of ways in which the novel can be read and discussed.

Thirdly, you will notice that not all the approaches outlined below can be simply combined, as there are in some cases contradictions between them. You have to make up your own mind, in such instances, what your position is.

(i) Textual approaches

By 'textual approaches' I mean those critical discussions of novels which restrict themselves to information gained from the actual texts of novels discussed. Of course this restriction can never be absolute – we have to take some knowledge of the world to a discussion of any novel in order to make sense of it – but textual critics concentrate on the actual words of the novel(s) they are studying rather than bringing what is called *extrinsic* information into their criticism. Textual critics thus pay little or no attention to biographical information about authors (including other writings by him or her), information about the author's society and historical period, the history of readers' responses to the novel, and so on. The relation between such a textual critic and the text of a novel is similar to that between a fundamentalist Christian and the Bible; all Christians of course treat the Biblical texts with respect as the source of wisdom and inspiration, but whereas some Christians suggest that the Bible has to be studied in its social and historical context, more fundamentalist Christians tend to read it 'in itself'.

Critics known as *formalists* take a particularly exclusivist attitude to the text. A formalist critic is one who pays great attention to the *form* of a literary work, but the term has been applied mostly to two groups of critics: the Russian formalists who wrote mainly in the 1920s, and the Anglo-American New Critics who flourished in the 1940s and 1950s. The New Critics – to oversimplify somewhat – rejected what they termed 'external' or 'extrinsic' information more or less *in toto*, preferring to concentrate upon 'the work itself' in relative isolation. In terms of *method* they often use what has been called *close reading* – taking a small section of a novel and reading this in exhaustive detail, drawing attention to the sort of things that I outlined in my earlier 'checklist' in the previous section.

Such critics have, by common consent, contributed enormously to our understanding of the complexity and subtlety of great works of fiction, moving us away from merely discursive discussion of plots and characters and demonstrating that the novel is as receptive to detailed analysis as is poetry. My section on 'Analysing fiction' could not have been written without the work of such critics. A recent example of such criticism is David Lodge's *Language of Fiction* (1966). Lodge's analysis of Charlotte Brontë's *Jane Eyre* in this work is a masterly isolation of patterns of reference and connotation in this novel, treating the novel almost as a poem that can be analysed in terms of its imagery as much as in terms of its plot and characters.

One important thing that such critics have reminded us of is that novels are *made*, they are not windows giving directly on to reality. They have thus led us to be much more wary about discussions of characters and events in novel that treat these as real people and happenings. A key influence here was L.C. Knights's essay 'How Many Children had Lady Macbeth?' (1933), which was concerned not with the novel but with drama. Knights was by no means a narrow formalist himself, but his essay has made critics aware of the dangers of referring to aspects of the life of characters in a literary work which take place 'outside of the text'.

This discussion has raised a crucial issue for readers of the novel. When we are immersed in, say, a novel by Dickens or Tolstoy, the characters are alive and real to us, and in our imagination they are as living people, their problems are human problems, and we experience emotions while reading which are comparable to the emotions aroused in us by real people and events.

We do not have to reject such imaginative experiences when we come to discuss a novel afterwards, but we do need to *complement* them with a sense of the novel as a creation, as something an author has crafted. Once we do this we will be led to realize that all sorts of *techniques* have been used by the writer to engender our sense of, and attitude to, the characters.

(ii) Generic approaches

A genre is a type or kind of literature, and we often refer to the novel itself as one of the three main literary genres along with poetry and drama. But there are many different ways to classify literature generically, and the novel has been divided into a number of sub-genres by various critics – which is what I myself did earlier on in this book when I spoke about 'Types of novel'. A generic approach to the novel insists that we cannot begin to read or understand a novel until we are clear as to what *sort* of novel it is – which for most critics means getting clear about the author's intentions with regard to his or her work. Thus – the argument goes – unless we understand the picaresque tradition within which Defoe's *Moll Flanders* is written we will run the danger of misreading and misunderstanding this novel.

This sort of initial orientation, of getting clear about what sort of work one is about to read, can often be one of the most useful benefits of reading critics. It is always a useful question to ask oneself once one is several pages into a novel whether one is clear as to what sort of novel it is. Sometimes an author may want to baffle and surprise a reader, but sometimes a modern reader may need the help of historical scholarship and criticism in order to get clarity on such matters.

(iii) Contextual approaches

If the most valuable aspect of the work of formalist critics has been their development of methods of critical analysis, the aspect of their work which has gone least unchallenged by others has been their rejection or near-rejection of 'extrinsic' information as an adjunct to the reading and criticism of literature.

Those who have advanced such challenges have argued that no utterance – including a literary work – can properly be understood independently of the context in which it was made and intended to be received. A sign reading 'All trains go to Victoria' makes perfectly good sense only when we understand that it is designed to be read in a particular context, and as it is usually firmly fixed in that context this is how it normally is read. But literary works are not screwed to the ground, and so we often need help to remind us of that context that has receded in time as the novel has been circulated to a range of new reading situations undreamt of by its author.

Sociological and *Marxist* critics have placed great stress upon the need to understand the context of the author's own society and his or her position within it, both as an individual (a member of a particular social group or class) and as an author (a member of a literary group, relying on certain publishers, libraries, readers, and so on).

Take Joseph Conrad's *Heart of Darkness*. Recent critics have suggested that the novella can only be fully appreciated in the context of what European powers were doing in Africa in the last part of the nineteenth century, and in particular in the context of statements made by prominent Belgians – including King Leopold – concerning the Belgian exploitation of the Congo (in which Conrad himself had worked). Thus some of Leopold's statements on the (extremely brutal and shocking) Belgian exploitation of the Congo include comments about opening to civilization the only part of our globe where Christianity has not penetrated, and piercing 'the darkness which envelops the entire population'. Conrad's ironic use of words such as 'civilization' and 'darkness' in the novella, it has been argued, can only fully be understood in the light of statements such as Leopold's.

But more than this, argue some contextual critics, is needed. The narrative indirection in the novel – Marlow's inability to tell the truth to Kurtz's 'Intended' and his feeling that he cannot make himself understood to his auditors – mirrors a situation in which comfortable Europeans who had never witnessed colonial brutality at first hand in Africa were unable to hear the truth spoken by such as Marlow.

This argument raises some problems in its turn. Conrad deliberately left out localizing information such as the name of the European country or the part of Africa in which the novella was set, and with regard to his short story 'Youth' he made it clear that he very much objected to having such information re-inserted.[14] It has been argued that the novella itself contains as much of this sort of contextualizing information as is needed. Key issues here are: what information is *relevant*? What information points to material that had a *determining* effect on the writing of the work?

Sociological critics have also drawn attention to the important influence that factors referred to collectively as the 'sociology of literature' can have on the creation of works of literature: publishers, patrons, literacy rates, readership profiles, libraries, booksellers, and so on. It is clear that if only a part of society is literate and can read novels, then this will affect the sort of novels that are written – as was the case in eighteenth-century England. And if success as a novelist depends upon having your work accepted by the circulating libraries, and these accept nothing that does not conform to a set of rigidly moralistic views – as was the case for much of the nineteenth century in Britain – then the reader should know this before he or she expresses dissatisfaction with the portrayal of sexual relationships in a nineteenth-century novel.

(iv) Biographical approaches

When we read a novel that we like very much our natural tendency is often to look for other works by the same author. The more books by the same novelist that we read, the more we become conscious of common or similar elements in them, and the more we begin to build up a picture of the man or woman behind the printed text, constructing an idea of his or her values, interests, and attitudes.

Such an interest in an author can lead us to want to know more about the person in question in his or her own right, and then we may start to read the novels in the light of what we have learned about the author – even in terms of what he or she has said about them explicitly.

Such a biographical approach to the study of the novel – reading fictional works with explicit reference to the life, personality, and opinions of the author – seems straightforward enough, yet it is fraught with problems and has involved many sharp debates. D.H. Lawrence advised: 'Never trust the artist. Trust the tale',[15] and generations of critics have pointed out that novelists *can* be very bad guides to their own work. Many of those works of Franz Kafka's that we prize today would have been burnt after his death had the author's wishes been carried out. Charles Dickens seems to have thought that the only defence of the 'spontaneous combustion' scene in *Bleak House* that needed to be made was that spontaneous combustion (of human beings!) was an established scientific fact. Joseph Conrad is a notoriously unreliable guide to his own novels both with regard to matters of fact and to matters of interpretation.

Why should this be so? We can isolate a number of possible explanations. Firstly that of *inspiration*. The writer seems often not to use the conscious and rational part of his or her mind for literary composition – something that has been appreciated since the days of antiquity when the term 'inspiration' was first used. So that secrets of the created work may not be accessible to the rational, enquiring mind in the same way that details of other actions and utterances are. Secondly that the author may want actually to *conceal* something: a real-life model, a confessional element in the work, or whatever. And thirdly the author may comment on his or her work a very long time after writing it.

When it is a matter of relating a novelist's work to his or her life then similar problems may emerge. How do we know which experiences in a writer's life were reflected (or transformed) in his or her work? Experiences which seem minor to us may have been crucial to the person who had them – but even so, they may not have influenced the writing of a given work.

If all this sounds like a counsel of despair I should add that it is not meant to be: I *do* think that biographical information can be of very great help in enabling us to respond more fully to a novel or a short story. But we should be fully aware of the problems involved in such critical procedures, and we need always to be sensitive to what the work itself can tell us.

Take D.H. Lawrence's novel *Women in Love*. It seems very

likely that Lawrence's experiences in the period of the First World War had a crucial effect on the writing of this novel even though the war is not mentioned at all in it (in spite of the fact that it was written in the middle of these experiences.) Lawrence was medically unfit for service in the war, and came under suspicion from the authorities because of his relationship with the German Frieda von Richthoven, who he married. He and Frieda were even forced to leave their cottage on the Cornish coast because they were suspected of signalling to German U-boats! Now although none of this is directly referred to in *Women in Love* it is arguable that much of the tone of that novel – in particular of its dismissive remarks about England – can only be fully understood in the light of these experiences of Lawrence's. Moreover, the comments in the novel by Birkin about the destructiveness of the 'mechanical principle' have, too, to be seen in the context of Lawrence's complex responses to the slaughter of the war – a slaughter that is not mentioned directly in the novel at all.

I stress that this sort of interpretation has to be handled with extreme tact and sensitivity, and it is a good idea to try to read and respond to a novel independently of such information first. If the information *then* seems to enable one to understand the work better or to clear up puzzles in one's own response then there is a better chance that one's interpretation is not doing too much violence to the work.

(iv) Psychological approaches

Biographical criticism can often shade off into psychological criticism: trying to use the work to uncover the psychology of its creator, and then to use any insights so gained to shed fresh illumination on the work. Psychological criticism can do more than this, however; it can involve psychological or psychoanalytic theories to analyse *characters* in a novel, or to analyse the *reader* in the light of his or her responses to it. Take Henry James's novella *The Turn of the Screw*. A succession of critics have psychoanalysed the governess in this tale, finding evidence of mental instability of a sort that leads her to hallucinate and to imagine the ghosts that she reports on to the reader.

The problem that this raises is similar to that about which I talked earlier: treating a literary character as if he or she were a real person. Can it make sense to talk about psychoanalysing a literary character? Does a literary character have an Unconscious? Of course an author can choose to create a character who behaves like a real person, even to the extent of having repressions or being mentally ill, but it seems rather dangerous to assume that an author can unconsciously create a character who has the same sort of psychic life as a real person. (Indeed, what sense does this sort of suggestion make?)

I think that we have to conclude that there is a stage in our reading of a novel when we treat the characters in it as real people in our imagination, but that this treatment can only go so far and has to be complemented by an analysis based on our understanding of them as creations of the author.

Using a novel or novels as a means to psychoanalyse an author meets fewer problems of this sort; the author is after all a real person, and if it is correct to see literary composition as in some ways akin to dreaming then we may assume that a novel can reveal at least as much about an author's psychic life as can a dream. Nevertheless, such attempts have not in general been found convincing by most readers. Joseph Conrad is a favourite subject for such psychoanalytic biographies which draw heavily on evidence contained in his works, but the general opinion of such attempts at understanding his psychology has been that they are at least highly contentious, asserting links between the works and the man which can at best represent only possible hypotheses.

(v) Reader-oriented approaches

If we were to indulge in a vast and only partly justified generalization we could say that criticism of the novel up to the 1930s was often highly *biographical* in tendency – talking about the author as much as if not more than his or her work; that from about this time onwards *textual* and *sociological* approaches to the study of the novel assumed a dominant importance (often in opposition to each other); and that over the past decade or so a growing interest in the *reader* and in the *reading process* can be detected.

Part of this can be explained as a reaction against New Critical treatments of the text of a novel as an object, an object that can be studied objectively. On the contrary, recent critics have pointed out, the reading of a novel is a *process*, and to treat a novel as an object obscures the fact that we experience a novel as a set of responses over time.

Other critics have suggest that it may well be misleading to talk of 'the reader' as if all readers (and readings) were the same. Virginia Woolf called a collection of her essays *The Common Reader* (1925), taking the phrase from Samuel Johnson and suggesting a respect for the ordinary as against the academic or specialist reader. But recent critics have started to talk of different conceptualizations of the reader: the implied reader, the original reader, the empirical reader.

The *implied reader* is that reader suggested by the text itself, most obviously when a narrator addresses comments directly to a reader but not only by such means. When Jane Austen's narrator builds up an intimate relationship with her reader she does it by making assumptions about the reader: his or her values, interests, understanding. We can say, then, that we can almost build up an 'identikit' picture of the reader of a Jane Austen novel – the reader that we actually become when we read the novel in the way it was intended to be read. Thus although two very different people may sit down to read *Emma*, in the process of reading that novel they may to some extent become very similar readers as they conform to the sort of reader that the novel implies it expects. (Think how we respond to what people expect us to be when they talk to us.) Of course the gap between what we are and what the novel seems to want us to become may be so wide that we rebel at the pressure to conform. In such a case we may give the novel what students of the mass media have termed an *oppositional reading* – a reading that asserts values, interests and understanding contrary to those that we feel are implied in the work.

The *original reader* is obviously a sort of fictive construct like that of the 'first-night audience' for a play. It involves an attempt to understand the novel in its historical context by asking what a sensitive, well-informed and intelligent reader would have made of the novel when first it was published. Note that this is not to say that an original reader is the same as an *ideal reader*; it may well be that later readers can see more in a novel than could have been seen on its first appearance. Many critics, without actually using the term, posit an ideal reader in their discussions of a novel: the reader who will respond in a way that maximalizes what the novel can offer.

I think that the problem with such an assumption is that no single reading of a novel can combine all of that which a novel can offer a reader. As I have already pointed out, we get different things from a first and a second reading of the same novel and it is hard to see, logically, how these could be combined.

Moreover readers from different backgrounds can hardly be expected to read the same novel in exactly the same way. When we turn to *empirical readers* we have to assume, I think, that an accountant will read *Sons and Lovers* differently from the way in which a coal-miner will read it. What exactly the nature of this difference will be it is hard to state precisely, and it is possible to make a case for its being a matter of details rather than of essentials. It is worth spending some time to analyse yourself as a reader however. To what extent are you likely to be influenced – even biased – in certain directions because of your background? Are there gaps in your knowledge or experience which may affect your understanding of this particular novel negatively? Can these be rectified in any way?

(vi) Feminist approaches

Just as feminists in society at large have encouraged us to look afresh at many aspects of our culture and history – down to quite small details of personal speech and behaviour – so too they have been extremely successful in getting us to look at literary works in new and often revealing ways. Over fifty years ago Virginia Woolf's *A Room of One's Own* (1929) startled readers by claiming that they lived in a patriarchy and that this fact conditioned the ways in which novels were written (or not written) and read. In more recent years a growing number of feminist critics have offered challenging accounts of the novel in general and of particular novels. Feminist critics have argued that not only have women had to overcome severe difficulties to become writers, but that once they have produced novels these have consistently been read in negative ways by male readers. Thus once a woman had managed to become literate (no easy matter in the past) she had to overcome all sorts of male prejudices in the reception accorded to her work. As Virginia Woolf expresses it:

This is an important book, the critic assumes, because it deals with war. This is an insignificant book because it deals with the feelings of women in a drawing-room.[16]

Moreover, as Woolf points out, it may be difficult for a woman to write about such things as war because of the domestic rôle to which she has been confined, and she declares that a woman could not have written *War and Peace*.

Feminist critics have also done much to show the ways in which male views of reality have dominated much fiction – especially, of course, that by men, and especially their views of women. Women are typically portrayed *in relation to men*, and are often seen in certain stereotyped ways – as passive, hysterical, emotional, 'bitch' or 'goddess'. Thus it seems fair to say that it is only as a result of the efforts of feminist critics in recent years that the portrayal of women in D.H. Lawrence's major novels has been questioned and criticized, and that many other authors have been looked at with new eyes.

If this has been the negative, devaluing side of feminist criticism its positive side has been the 'rediscovery' or reinstatement of a number of (mainly women) writers whose works have been undervalued or forgotten. A number of publishing imprints devoted to encouraging the publication of works by women – both new authors and authors from the past – have been established, and the present high reputations of writers such as Jean Rhys, Doris Lessing, Tillie Olsen and others owe much (if not most) to the efforts of feminist critics.

In the past decade or so critical movements with the titles of *structuralist*, *post-structuralist* and *deconstructionist* have achieved considerable renown – or notoriety. Within the scope of a short book such as this it is not possible to give a summary of such developments that would do them justice or give the reader anything like an adequate summary of their essential features. Readers interested in finding out more about them are advised to consult the recommendations concerning further reading.

Notes

[1]Ian Watt, *The Rise of the Novel* (Harmondsworth, Penguin Books, 1963), p. 14.

[2]Charles Stokes Carey (ed.), *Letters Written by Lord Chesterfield to his Son* (London, Wm. Reeves, 1912), volume 1, p. 90 (Original letter in French). The letter is undated but is probably written around 1740–41.

[3]Arnold Kettle, *An Introduction to the English Novel* (London, Hutchinson, 1951), volume 1, p. 22.

[4]Ralph Fox, *The Novel and the People* (London, Lawrence and Wishart, reprinted 1979), p. 44.

[5]Samuel Richardson, *Clarissa: Or, the History of a Young Lady* (London, Dent, reprinted 1962), volume 4, p. 81.

[6]C.T. Watts (ed.), *Joseph Conrad's Letters to R.B. Cunninghame Graham* (London, Cambridge University Press, 1969), p. 60.

[7]G. Jean-Aubry, *Joseph Conrad: Life and Letters* (New York, Doubleday Page, 1927), volume 1, p. 303.

[8]Francis Wyndham & Diana Melly (eds.), *Jean Rhys: Letters 1931–1966* (London, André Deutsch, 1984), p. 162.

[9]op cit, p. 172.

[10]Christopher Isherwood, *Christopher and his Kind: 1929–1939* (London, Methuen, 1977), pp. 141–42.

[11]Jean Rhys, *Good Morning, Midnight* (Harmondsworth, Penguin Books, reprinted 1969), p. 101.

[12]James Joyce, *Ulysses* (Harmondsworth, Penguin Books, reprinted with corrections 1971), p. 85.

[13]I discuss the resemblances between these two novels in more detail in my *Multiple Personality and the Disintegration of Literary Character* (London, Edward Arnold, 1983), p. 91. I refer to similarities between the *plots* of the novels however, whereas strictly speaking I should have referred to similarities between their *stories*.

[14]In a letter to Richard Curle: see Richard Curle (ed.), *Conrad to a Friend: 150 Selected Letters from Joseph Conrad to Richard Curle* (London, Sampson Low, Marston and Company, 1928), pp. 142–3.

[15]D.H. Lawrence, 'The Spirit of Place', in Antony Beal (ed.), *Selected Literary Criticism: D.H. Lawrence* (London, Mercury Books, 1961), p. 297.

[16]Virginia Woolf, *A Room of One's Own* (London, Hogarth Press, reprinted 1967), p. 111.

Further Reading

Always try to ensure that you are not reading a novel in an inferior text. Many quite widely circulated paperback works have less than ideal texts, and it is possible to read a novel such as *Wuthering Heights* in a modern edition but in a form other than that which the author intended. The Penguin and World's Classics (Oxford University Press) texts maintain a high standard of textual reliability in the main, and the latter series includes critical introductions and notes as standard features. If you can afford them, the Norton Critical Editions are the ideal, with excellent texts and a selection of important critical material in each volume. Teachers and lecturers do not much like those 'Notes' that are little more than extended cribs, with plot summaries carefully provided for those who cannot be bothered to read the texts themselves. In some of these the critical comments are extremely bad. The best of this sort of series is the 'York Notes' one, published by Longman. These are all written by very reputable scholars, and can be relied upon.

Other useful and reliable critical series are the Macmillan Casebooks, the Prentice-Hall Twentieth-Century Views and Twentieth-Century Interpretations, and the Studies in English Literature published by Edward Arnold. The New Accents series published by Methuen contains many interesting works, although not all of them are as accessible as one might wish.

In addition, the following individual works can all be recommended.

Wayne C. Booth, *The Rhetoric of Fiction* (Chicago, University of Chicago Press, 1961).
    A book that really initiated the new wave of interest in narrative technique. Booth is a stimulating and accessible

critic, and his book has been enormously influential. The second edition contains an interesting 'Afterword'.

Malcolm Bradbury (ed.), *The Novel Today: Contemporary Writers on Modern Fiction* (Fontana, Glasgow, 1977).
A very useful collection of essays by practising novelists writing about their own, and others', fiction. Essential for any student interested in modernism and post-modernism in the novel.

Peter Brooks, *Reading for the Plot: Design and Intention in Narrative* (Clarendon Press, Oxford, 1984).
A more advanced book, demanding but not inaccessible. Contains challenging analyses of *Le Rouge et le Noir, Great Expectations, Heart of Darkness*, and Faulkner's *Absalom, Absalom!*

Dorrit Cohn, *Transparent Minds: Narrative Modes for Presenting Consciousness in Fiction* (Princeton, Princeton University Press, 1978).
Now available in paperback, this is, again, an advanced and demanding work, but it is exhaustive in its coverage of its topic: how do novelists present characters' consciousnesses in their fiction? Deserves to be read in full, but can be 'dipped into' for specific information.

E.M. Forster, *Aspects of the Novel* (London, Edward Arnold, 1927).
Now available in a convenient Penguin edition, this is still hard to better as a discursive introduction to the novel; disarmingly unsophisticated and straightforward, but nonetheless packed with valuable observations.

Jeremy Hawthorn (ed.), *Narrative: From Malory to Motion Pictures* (London, Edward Arnold, 1985).
Contains a range of essays applying recent narrative theory to particular texts. The second and third essays are of particular interest to anyone interested in studying the immediate ancestors of the novel.

Arnold Kettle, *An Introduction to the English Novel* (London, Hutchinson, volume one 1951, volume two 1953).
A critical work that has, deservedly, become a standard text. Kettle provides a thought-provoking introduction to the historical antecedents of the novel, but the heart of the

book lies in its sensitive and intelligent analyses of individual texts, analyses which are never narrow but which encompass a range of historical and moral issues.

Mary Jacobus (ed.), *Women Writing and Writing about Women* (London, Croom Helm, 1979).
One of the best of the many recent books on literature written from a feminist perspective (or set of perspectives). Contains essays concerned with Charlotte Brontë, George Eliot, Virginia Woolf, Thomas Hardy, and others.

Ann Jefferson and David Robey (eds.), *Modern Literary Theory: A Comparative Introduction* (London, Batsford Academic, 1982).
One of the best of the many recent guides to modern literary theory. This is, however, not an easy book, mainly because the theories with which it is concerned are so complex. Any reader seeking further information on structuralism could do much worse than to start here though.

F.R. Leavis, *The Great Tradition* (London, Chatto & Windus, 1948).
Along with Leavis's other books concerned with the novel (*D.H. Lawrence, Novelist* [London, Chatto and Windus, 1955], and *Dickens the Novelist* [London, Chatto and Windus, 1970] – which was written jointly with his wife Q.D. Leavis) this represents a critical account of the novel which is highly exclusivist (some have said élitist) but which includes marvellously insightful and sensitive commentaries on major novels.

David Lodge, *Language of Fiction* (London, Routledge, 1966).
Along with Lodge's other literary-critical books this can be strongly recommended for its highly revealing textual analyses. The study of *Jane Eyre* it contains is an object lesson in what close textual analysis of a novel can reveal. The introductory section on problems in criticism of the novel is a fine starting point for consideration of the criticism of the novel.

Shlomith Rimmon-Kenan, *Narrative Fiction: Contemporary Poetics* (London, Methuen, 1983).
This is the most accessible introduction to recent developments in narrative theory. ('Poetics', incidentally, has nothing specifically to do with poetry, but means a systematized theory – after Aristotle's *Poetics*).

Martin Seymour-Smith, *Novels and Novelists: A Guide to the World of Fiction* (New York, St Martin's Press, 1980).

Although this has the outward appearance of a coffee-table book, and its 'star-ratings' of major novels may strike a discordant note, it actually contains some excellent sections written by highly respected academics. Seymour-Smith himself provides a splendid opening chapter on the origins and development of the novel, J.A. Sutherland provides chapters on approaches to the novel and the novel and the book trade, Gāmini Salgādo writes on the novelist at work, Michael Mason on fiction and illustration, and David Pirie contributes a thought-provoking chapter on the novel and the cinema.

Mark Spilka (ed.), *Towards a Poetics of Fiction* (Bloomington and London, Indiana University Press, 1977).

This book contains essays from the journal *Novel* from the period 1967–1976, and includes many fine theoretical and interpretative pieces by well-known writers. Wayne C. Booth and Ian Watt comment, respectively, on their influential books *The Rhetoric of Fiction* and *The Rise of the Novel*. There are also studies of the criticism of Georg Lukács, Wayne C. Booth, and F.R. Leavis, and an essay on the contributions of formalism and structuralism to the theory of fiction. This is a major source for ideas about the novel, not simple, but well worth study.

Dorothy Van Ghent, *The English Novel: Form and Function* (New York, Rinehart & Company, 1953).

Now available in a convenient paperback edition, this is probably the major New Critical contribution to the study of the novel. Its close analyses of individual texts, and its clarity and perception, make it a very useful student textbook.

Ian Watt, *The Rise of the Novel* (London, Chatto & Windus, 1957).

Now available in a Penguin edition this is the classic study of the emergence and development of the English novel in the eighteenth century. Recent research has qualified some of Watt's arguments, but his analyses of *Robinson Crusoe, Moll Flanders, Pamela, Clarissa*, and *Tom Jones* are still essential reading.

Index